The Legend of Suzy High Kick

Wm. BARNARD

authorHOUSE®

AuthorHouse™
1663 Liberty Drive
Bloomington, IN 47403
www.authorhouse.com
Phone: 833-262-8899

Published by AuthorHouse 10/27/2020

ISBN: 978-1-6655-0437-9 (sc)
ISBN: 978-1-6655-0436-2 (e)

This book is dedicated to the loving memory of my Granny Bs. Special thank you to Gloria McCain, Justin Parker, and the countless teachers who pour out their lives into helping kids with disabilities.

Chapter 1

August 21

The soft orange rays of sunrise poured through the middle gap of the curtains, filling the room with the warmth of a new day. There was a quiet stillness in the room and the morning light revealed a predominantly pink color scheme, including the twin bed frame, blankets, and pillows. Pink walls are lined with posters of boy band stars who keep watch over their greatest fan who is sleeping in the bed below.

On top of an oak nightstand, oddly *not* painted pink, sat an alarm clock resembling a small juke box. At exactly 6:30 AM, the juke box came to life with a rainbow of colors flashing across its clear bubble top. The small speakers blared the classic hit from the Fifties, 'Wake up Little Susie'.

> "Whatta we gonna tell your mama, Whatta we gonna tell your pa
>
> Whatta we gonna tell our friends, when they say ooh-la-laâ
>
> Wake up little Susie, wake up. Wake up little Susie, wake up."

But little Suzy in the bed next to the juke box did not wake up. She didn't even flinch. She continued to live up to one of her many nicknames, Miss Snuzy.

Lying on her back, snoring loudly, Suzy's right arm was bent around her head, her hand almost touching the other shoulder. Her low muscle tone is typical for Down Syndrome kids and this flexibility enables her to sleep in a variety of crazy positions that would make a cat enviable.

The bedroom light overhead flipped on as her half asleep Dad lumbered into the room. He was not surprised that the new alarm clock had no effect whatsoever on her.

"Wake up little Snuzy, wake up," Brian sang. He reached down and tickled her exposed underarm and Suzy merely grunted.

"Come on kid, first day of your big Senior year. Time to get up and slay the day."

Rolling on to her side and trying to ignore his plea, she mumbled, "Dad, I'm sleeping."

"I know you are. I am standing right here watching you. But you have to get up." Brian leaned in, grabbing the hand of the contorted arm and brought it into a more natural position.

Suzy's eyes fluttered open, but Brian knew his battle was not nearly over. While he is a fit 6 foot, 200 pound grown man, his baby girl was not so little anymore. Her thyroid problem had led to an increase in weight, putting her near 120 pounds. Picking her up was no longer a simple task.

Brian continued to try to prod her awake. "What happened? You were all excited last night, dancing around all crazy about going back to school."

"I know, but I was awake then," Suzy unknowingly deadpanned. It is these little Suzyisms that keep her Dad smiling.

"Ok, so you can just stay home, and I can find you some chores. You've always dreamed of cutting the grass, right?" Brian tried his reverse psychology approach.

"No. I have school. You cut the grass. That's your job, Dad."

"Then get up, let's go." Brian pulled his daughter up to her feet before heading to the kitchen. Suzy dressed herself in a yellow sundress with white running shoes, but her mother had to come in to help braid her hair into two pigtails. They both looked at each other in the reflection of the stand-up mirror in Suzy's room.

The only resemblance Suzy has to her mother is her black hair, long eye lashes and brown eyes. And a radiating smile.

Suzy is just under five feet tall with a stocky frame and has a cute, round face. Her mother is almost a foot taller than Suzy, slender with very defined facial bone structure.

"Look at mi hija, muy bonita," Maria said, kissing Suzy on the cheek. "Hurry up to the living room. Papa is waiting for you."

While walking out together to the bus stop on the corner of their neighborhood street, Brian asked, "Suzy, how do you sleep like that, with your arm all twisted around your head?" He tried to cartoonishly imitate her, looking very apish. She glanced at him quickly, still too sleepy to laugh. Brian continued, "The Doctor explained it to me once, but it still doesn't make sense."

"I don't know, Dad," she replied just as the bus pulls up. "It's just one of my skills."

"Yes, just one of many sweetheart." Brian reached down and kissed her on the forehead.

The bus doors folded open and Suzy's bus driver for the past 3 years greeted her with a huge grin on his face. At 6'4 with a 250-pound muscle bound frame, Henry Jackson is an imposing figure. Driving a bus for special needs kids helped him with his PTSD after his combat tour years ago in the Middle East. His short afro is almost all gray, but it has been that way since the war.

"Well, well, well. If it is not the Queen of Gilmerton herself," Henry proclaimed.

"How come you said I was the Queen of Georgia last year, Henry?" Suzy asked after stopping at the top step.

"That's because you are both, Suzy." Henry smiled, giving her a high five as she walks back to her seat.

"Nice recovery, Henry." Brian reached up, extending a handshake to the driver.

"She always keeps me on my toes. I'm looking forward to seeing what this new year brings. Have a blessed day, Brian."

"You, too. Henry. I pray God's safety over you and these kids."

"Thank you, kindly." Henry smiled while closing the doors.

The four-mile trip to West End High School is scenic, one of the reasons Brian and his wife Maria decided to move twelve years ago from Atlanta to this small, North Georgia town. At the foothills of the Appalachian Mountains, the lush green forest that surrounded the town would soon be providing a color kaleidoscope of red, yellow and orange leaves in autumn.

For some reason, there are only two other kids on the bus this morning and both are asleep. Suzy wanted to talk to her classmates, but instead she just nestled into her seat and let them doze. As the small yellow bus weaved thru the curves, Suzy peered out her window, recognizing the jogger with the purple hoodie who ran along the road. Her Brother Daniel ran to school every day and even though he could not see into the bus because of the glare off the window, he waved anyway. She waved back thinking he could actually see her. By the time the bus slowly crossed over a single lane metal bridge over the Coosawattee river, Suzy drifted back into dream land.

"Ok, kids. We are here. This is your Big Day. First Day of School!" Henry announced loudly as the air brakes of the bus hissed, startling the kids awake.

Waiting outside the bus to assist the kids were two Special Ed teacher aides who can help them find their new classes. Marco assisted Justin off the back of the bus in his wheelchair, escorting him and Katie.

Heather, a small, petite blond woman in her early twenties who had been tutoring Suzy the last two years, greeted her with a big hug as she exited the bus.

"Hey there old friend. I missed you!" Heather exclaimed.

"I missed you, too. Why didn't you come to my birthday?"

"Oh sorry, Suz. I was outta town. Did you have fun without me?

"Yes. We had lots of cake."

"What? You were supposed to say no, I couldn't have fun without you." Heather laughed.

Changing her voice into a deep and serious tone, Suzy replied, "You're crazy, Heather."

"You're not the only one who says that, Suz."

"I know."

Heather shook her head. "You are too, funny, kiddo."

"My dad tells me that all the time. You come next year birthday, ok?" Suzy insisted and looked at Heather for confirmation.

"Definitely I will be there. But right now, I'm looking forward to teaching you some new recipes I learned this summer. Does that sound fun?"

"Oh yeah! Can't wait. Is Mister Billy here?" Suzy asked about her teacher.

"Maybe. You will just have to wait." Heather teased Suzy, knowing Billy would indeed be there.

The Bus drop-off was in front of the basketball arena, and as the kids and aides rounded the gym on the sidewalk, there was a small group of cheerleaders having an impromptu practice on the adjacent grass.

Suzy slowed down; her eyes transfixed on them. She would have been content to stay here all day and gaze at their every move. The girls were dressed in sweatpants and t-shirts and Suzy wondered why they were not wearing their Cheerleading uniforms. If Suzy owned one, she would wear it everywhere.

Heather put her arm around Suzy, nudging her forward and saying, "Come on, Suz. We gotta get you to your new classroom."

Bobbing his head back and forth to the funky rhythm of The Clash's 'Magnificent Seven' on full blast in his ear buds, Billy Martin made his way down the hallway lined with school lockers to his classroom of seniors. He could almost pass for a senior himself with his baby face, curly brown hair and carefree attitude. He rarely opts for anything but his usual attire of blue jeans, flannel shirt and Chuck Taylor Converse and this day was no exception.

You'd be forgiven if you misjudged his intellect based on his appearance. But Billy Martin graduated from Furman University on an academic scholarship in only three years. He quickly returned to his hometown five years ago to teach Special Ed and has been honored as a top teacher in the State of Georgia.

Billy entered the classroom just as the school bell rings, sliding across the vinyl floor at the front of the class. He grabbed some white chalk and wrote in huge letters on the clean, black board, 'The Magnificent Seven!'

Taking off his ear buds, he exclaimed, "What's up my people!"

There is laughter among the small class and a smattering of "Hi, Teacher, Hi, Mister Billy."

Pointing toward the chalkboard behind him, Billy said, "Do you know who the Magnificent Seven is?"

The kids glanced at each other with quizzical looks, remaining quiet.

Billy threw his hands in the air and exclaimed, "You are! You are the Magnificent Seven!"

Sitting on the front row in his wheelchair, Justin Graham's eyes darted from his side to side. He raised his hand and then blurted out quickly, "Mister Billy, there are only six kids in our class." Despite his autism, Justin doesn't do just simple arithmetic, but finished college level calculus as a sophomore. "Who is the seventh one?" Justin asked.

"Well, me, of course. I am number seven. Billy da Kid!"

The other kids laughed out loud, but Justin looked up at the ceiling, perplexed and appearing to go over his calculations in his head again.

"Guys, remember I told you to be thinking over the summer of what your dreams are for this year? Now we are going to go around the room and each one of you is going to tell us what your number one dream is, ok?"

Billy approached Justin first who was wearing a Star Wars baseball cap and a t-shirt with the famous character of the same movie, Yoda, on it. "Mister Justin, what is your dream?"

"I want to be a Jedi. Like Obi Wan Kenobi in Star Wars."

"What? No way. I would have never guessed that. That's an awesome dream because you are awesome. May the force be with you." Billy placed his right fist into the open palm of his left hand before bowing at his waist while Justin nodded back.

Sitting directly behind Justin is Josh Manford. With dark complexion and a stout frame, Josh's Down Syndrome features don't stand out nearly as much as his punk rock ensemble. This week it was purple hair and this day was a Dead Kennedy's t-shirt, and leather arm bands with fake metal studs on them.

"So, Josh, what is your big dream?" Billy asked.

"I wanna be a punk rocker," Josh said with a big smile.

"Josh, you are living the dream. Well, as a wise sage said once, 'do the worm on the acropolis, slam dance the cosmopolis, enlighten the populace," Billy finished before bowing to Josh.

Beside Josh sat Katie McClure, who wore glasses with lenses that resemble the bottom of coke bottles, long blonde hair and also has Down Syndrome.

Clasping his hands in front of his face, Billy said, "Miss Katie, I cannot wait to hear your dream."

"Mister Billy, I want to run hair salon. With my mom. I will cut your long hair."

"That is magnificent. Many people do say I need professional help. Can you please give me a pedicure too?

Katie stuck out her tongue and scrunched her face. "No, that's gross. I am not gonna touch your feet Mister Billy!" Her comment and facial expression made all the kids laugh.

Billy got on one knee before her and started using an English accent, "Fair enough, Miss Katie, I now dub thee, Miss Scissor Hands." Katie did not get the reference to the movie which Billy quickly realized was not a bad thing.

Earl Smith, a tall, lanky boy with black hair and mustache fuzz sits at an angle in his chair. Diagnosed with autism at 4 years old, he leaned into the row next to him, swiveling his head continuously.

Billy moved over and sat on the empty desk next to Earl, maintaining the English Accent and said, "Sir Earl, what is it that thou aspireth to do?"

"Huh?" Earl asked with a blank face, obviously confused by the accent and King James English.

"What is your dream, Earl?" Billy restated in his normal voice.

"To be the best dancer in the whole school," Earl declared. He promptly stood up, busting a quick jig before sitting down abruptly.

Shocked, Billy stood with his mouth ajar. Three years ago, Earl barely spoke during class and rarely showed much emotion. Billy hoped this dance was a sign that Earl may be coming out of his shell.

"That. Was. Incredible! You just absolutely blew my mind, Mister Earl!" Billy said before switching into the voice of singer James Brown. "You jumped back, kissed yourself and got down with yo' bad self."

Billy shook his head in disbelief before repeating the bowing tradition.

Still chuckling and smiling from Earl's dance move, Buster Moore enthusiastically awaited his favorite teacher. Buster has red hair and his round face is covered in freckles and he also has Downs. He usually wears a T-shirt that has one word in giant print across the front. This day the shirt read 'Truth'.

"Okay Mister Buster, how about it? What's your big dream?

"I wanna be a Preacher!" Buster exclaimed, thrusting his hand toward the heavens.

"Yes, you are gonna be busting out the Bible and telling people about the love of Jesus! Can I get a witness? Somebody bettah testify up in here!" Billy placed his hands together in prayer position and bowed to his student before saying, "Bless you, Mister Buster."

"God bless you, Mister Billy." Buster smiled.

Billy cupped his hands to amplify his voice, going into game announcer mode.

"Well, last but not least, a lady who needs no further introduction, the one that is internationally known on the microphone, The. Miss. Suzzzyyy! Now don't keep us in suspense any longer, what is your big dream?"

Grabbing one of her pigtails, Suzy proclaimed, "I wanna be a Cheerleader!"

Billy immediately started up a cheer, "Her name is Suzy, she takes no flack, you mess with Suzy, bettah watch your back!"

The cheer caused Suzy to spontaneously get out of her chair, performing a high kick and coming within a foot of hitting Billy in the chest.

Billy hopped backwards with his hands up in a defensive Karate stance and in a Japanese accent said, "Oh, I see your Taekwondo game is on point, girl." Billy placed his right fist into the other empty palm and bowed to Suzy who giggled in return.

"Okay, I loved hearing all y'all's dreams and look forward to seeing them come true. This year we are going to focus on your life skills. We will be continuing to do outings downtown, learning how to buy things and counting money. We will also be learning to cook things like pancakes, pizza, burritos and mixing up some smoothies. And we will learn to clean up the Home Ec room which should make some of your parents' dreams come true. But right now, class is dismissed, and you can go to P.E."

Buster leaned over to Suzy and joked that he was glad the class was over, "Praise the Lord!"

"I heard that Buster," Billy said, trying to give him a look of admonishment.

"Hold it! Stop!" Sherry Tinsdale screamed inside the basketball gym. The cheerleader coach threw her hands in the air before resting them on her head. "What am I even watching? It looks like you guys don't even care. Where is the energy? The first game of the season is this Friday and y'all look like you haven't practiced for the last three weeks."

The Captain of the team, Amanda, glanced over at her best friend Kylie, who rolled her eyes.

"Amanda, this is your squad. Get it together. I'm gonna get some coffee and when I get back, I want to see a different attitude. Look up at those banners. Three times National Champs, Five times Runner-Up. You seniors were on that Championship squad. You have a legacy to live up to. Now get on it!"

Sherry had been at West End High School for eight years now, teaching American and World History. Married to the Biology teacher and Basketball coach Dave Tinsdale, she looked young and fit enough to still be cheerleading at the University of Florida.

Not wanting any of that stale coffee in the teachers' lounge, she decided to drive to a nearby Starbucks.

Walking up to her red Mazda sports car, she noticed a man slowly riding a Harley motorcycle up to her reserved parking spot. When he stopped the bike, turned it off, and removed his helmet, she recognized the Special Ed teacher, Billy. She always thought he came across as a peculiar character in the few times she interacted with him around school. Nice, but odd.

"Hi Coach Sherry. I was hoping I could have a minute to ask you something."

"Uh, yeah, sure. But I am kinda in a hurry." She rifled through her purse and found her keys.

"Oh, I will be quick. Do you know the girl in my class, Suzy? She has Down Syndrome."

"Hmmm. Not sure. The blonde girl with glasses?"

"No, the other one. She's got brown hair. Usually has pigtails. Super funny."

"She's never been in any of my classes so no. What's up?" She said, putting her key in the door.

"Well, she told me today her dream is to be a Cheerleader. I was hoping you could let her come and join the team."

"Um… You do realize I had to cut over forty girls at tryouts for the team. This isn't just some club. These girls compete on a National level."

Billy scratched his head. This was not going as he had hoped. "Oh, I know you guys are great. I just thought she would bring, I don't know, a different element."

"Well, it's physically and mentally demanding to get these girls to perform at this level. It's very time consuming as well. I don't even feel the team is really ready for Friday night's game. I just don't see how we could fit her in right now."

Billy looked down and bit his lip. The pause allowed Sherry to open the car door quickly, sit down and say, "But I'll let you know if something changes."

After putting his black helmet on, Billy cranked up his Sportster, not looking over toward Sherry as he didn't want her to see the burning resentment in his eyes.

Billy Martin could be successful at anything he tried. His intellect and charm would take him far in the business world if he were ever to apply. But he loved these special needs kids. He was extremely invested in them, and nothing incensed him more than when others wouldn't give these kids a chance. He sped out of the parking lot, opting for the long way home and hoping the night air would help make his anger subside.

Coach Sherry arrived at her 3-bedroom house shortly after nine. She lagged coming home on purpose because her husband had left her a voice mail saying he wanted to have a talk. She loved Dave and knew he was trying to help, but also knew talking would only lead to dwelling more on what already troubled her.

The house looked essentially dark except for the flickering light the TV emanated against the living room walls. She cracked the front door quietly, hoping Dave had passed out on the couch. When the door creaked as she opened it more, she noticed Dave's head pop up from the couch.

"Hey honey, were you asleep?" Sherry said softly.

"No, just watching the regularly scheduled bad news. I got some Chinese takeout if you want me to heat it up." Dave flipped the TV off which signaled to Sherry that he wanted her to join him on the couch.

Deciding to divert the conversation to something trivial, she moved over to the adjacent dining room to put down her purse, saying, "Oh, thanks.

I'm not actually hungry. Hey, do you know that Special Ed teacher Billy something? He approached me about letting one of his Down Syndrome kids join the team. I mean, does he have any clue how complicated Cheer is these days? It takes all my time just to get these girls ready to go, never mind all the extra time it would take to acclimate her."

Since Sherry remained standing in the dining room, Dave stood up and walked over to within a few feet of her, rubbing the back of his neck uncomfortably. "Well, that's sorta what I wanted to talk about?" Dave said.

"What? The Down Syndrome girl?" Sherry tilted her head perplexed.

"No. All the time you spend working. After teaching all day, you spend the rest of the day on cheer. Then the entire weekend you are teaching gymnastics. You're just go, go, go."

"I know. But there isn't anyone else in this town that is qualified to really teach gymnastics. I am the only one who is accomplished and can help these girls get to the next level."

"Well, I'm worried about you. I'm worried you are burning the candle at both ends."

"I'll be fine, hon." She looked inside her purse, pretending to look for something.

"And… I'm worried about us," he said, trying to establish eye contact.

Sherry folded her arms in front of her. "What about you? Once basketball season starts, you will be busy coaching."

"Yes, but you go to those games, too, so at least we are there together." He put his hands in his back-jeans pockets.

"You are on the bench with your team. I am in the stands. It's not like we are exactly together."

"And that's what I wanted to tell you. I am willing to step down from coaching so we can be together more. I feel like we are becoming too dang busy. We need to have us."

"Babe, can we talk about this later. I'm just so burned out from the first day of school and I have to fill out a form and email it to the DOS office tonight."

He stepped forward and gave her a hug. She wrapped her arms around him and kissed him on the cheek before stepping away. "I need to fill out that form before my eyes can't see anymore. Is the computer on in the office?"

"I'm not sure," Dave said, realizing he was not just talking about the computer. Frustrated that he didn't know what his wife was really thinking, he headed back to the couch. He wanted to be able to get her to open up, but how to do that still eluded him. And while he didn't really know what to say to his wife at this point, he also wasn't sure that even if he did, whether he would really get a straight answer from her. So, he flipped the TV back on and stared at the screen, not hearing anything the newscaster said.

Making her way down the hallway, Sherry hurried past the first door on the right, wanting to avoid that room at all cost.

The next door on the right leads into the makeshift office where Sherry found it almost completely dark, the only light coming from the computer screen. At the small open desk, she flipped on the adjacent lamp before sitting down to fill out the online form and email it to the Director of the School District. The entire task only took ten minutes and after finishing it, Sherry was left staring at the wall in front of her, confronted with what is in the adjacent room.

She didn't want to think about it, but she simply couldn't help but think about it.

Every. Single. Day.

Sherry pictured the darkness in the other room, realizing it mirrored what it felt like in her own heart. She knew if she could reach through the wall, she would touch the empty crib, reminding her that the dream of having her own family had spiraled into a never-ending nightmare.

The miscarriage two years ago was painful. The second one seven months ago was somehow even more devastating. Since then, Sherry stopped asking God, "Why?" In fact, she stopped talking to God at all.

Suddenly Sherry bolted up out of her chair and turned the computer off. She tried to think of something that needed to be done so she rushed off to the laundry room, wanting to find refuge in staying occupied. By going thru the motions of menial tasks, she hoped one day the ache in her heart would finally end.

Chapter 2

Brian lay in bed awake but kept his eyes closed, hoping he could go back to sleep. But then he heard the alarm music of "Wake up Lil Susie" from his daughter's adjacent room.

"Wake up Lil Daddy, wake up," Suzy sang, causing Brian to open his eyes and see Suzy one foot from his face. She laughed before jumping on top of him and rolling over in between Maria and him.

"Group hug!" She exclaimed. Maria and Brian knew the drill well. They both rolled over to embrace Suzy and began kissing her on her cheeks.

"Wow. You're up early today," Maria said.

"I'm excited. We are going on field trip in community. I need ten dollars."

"Whoa, ten dollars. You need to clean the house little lady," Brian half joked.

"No, I don't. I need ten dollars!" Suzy was not a fan of housecleaning, but she surprised her parents once in a while when she cleaned up without any prompting from them.

"We need you to help out, Suz. I will give you ten dollars if you clean the living room," Brian insisted

Suzy rolled over to Maria. "Mom, can I have ten dollars?"

"Of, course mi reina." Calling Suzy her 'queen' in Spanish, Maria kissed her on the nose.

Brian lifted his head above Suzy and glanced at Maria, wishing she would back him up and help teach Suzy more about cleaning; but Maria loved to spoil her girl.

Later when Brian was brushing his teeth, Maria gave Suzy the money, watching her put it in the backpack.

As they walked out to the bus stop, Brian grabbed his daughter's hand. He loved how she never got tired of hugging them and unlike most teenagers, Suzy never got embarrassed when her Dad held her hand in public.

"Where are you going on your field trip, Snoozer?"

"The store. And to eat." Suzy rubbed her belly.

"What store? Are you getting me lunch?" Brian joked.

"No. We are going to Target. I'll get you gum, Dad."

"Make sure it's Bubble gum. Let me give you the ten dollars," Brian said, reaching for his wallet in his back pocket.

Neglecting to mention to Brian that mom had given her money moments earlier, Suzy took the ten-dollar bill and exclaimed, "I'm rich!"

About mid-morning, a school cargo van drove the special needs kids to downtown Gilmerton which looked like many other small, quaint Southern towns. There was a downtown square area with a park between the buildings and a green and white gazebo in the center. An assortment of tall Hickories, Green Ash and Holly trees provided a canopy of shade over the park benches and sidewalks. Facing each side of the square were two-story buildings that held shops and restaurants. Most of the structures were pre-1920s, and solid red brick. The iron lampposts that lined the square looked antique, but were actually recent additions and added a calming glow at night.

Remaining on Main Street past the Square, a row of Victorian style homes lined both sides of the two-lane road. The historic town feel ended abruptly only a half mile from the Square where a stucco strip mall appeared. The locals called it the Target Center despite the dozen other nationwide chains inside the complex.

After piling out of the van, the teachers escorted the kids single file down a sidewalk to the Target, with aide Heather leading in front and Billy rounding up the back. Last in the line of the kids, Suzy pushed Justin in his wheelchair as she was so fond of doing.

Suddenly Suzy yelled at her fellow student, "Hey, Buster!" trying to get his attention even though he was only a few feet in front of her.

Buster stopped walking and turned back to face Suzy, with his hands on his chubby waistline and his tongue protruding slightly from his mouth. His purple single word T-shirt read, Hope. "Hey, Suzy," he replied, thinking she was simply greeting him.

Known for his charismatic presence at First Baptist of Gilmerton, you will find Buster every Sunday, front and center, raising and waving his hands in praise. While the congregation preferred to worship conservatively, never singing louder than the person next to them, most of them had grown up with Buster and were accustomed to his "enthusiasm".

Suzy said smiling, "My dad said he always hears you at church cause you're the loudest singer."

Buster paused, blinking rapidly out of habit and took the statement as a compliment. "Well, tell him I said, thank you very much."

"Okay, I will," Suzy said.

Not trying to be mean, Suzy's Dad Brian joked with his family after church in the car ride home about Buster's style, causing them all to laugh. He didn't think she would share his comment to her whole classroom, but Suzy had been eager to tell Buster what her Dad had said.

Continuing down the sidewalk and nearing the entrance, they saw a homeless lady sat on a bench, clutching a green plastic bag under her arm. In her other hand, she held the leash to a brown Labrador mix who lay at her feet.

Suzy stopped pushing Justin's wheelchair in front of the bench. "What's your dog's name?

"Lucy." The lady answered, smiling that someone seemed to care about Lucy besides herself. She looked mid-forties, dark complexion with tangled brown hair.

"Can I pet him?" Suzy asked with her hand now hovering over the dog's head.

"Sure. It's a she, honey. And she loves to be petted." Alice leaned over and stroked the side of her pet.

"Good doggy. Are you hungry, Lucy?" Suzy said, rubbing the dog's ears. Turning to her side, she said, "Mister Billy, I am going to go buy Lucy a snack."

"Ok, Suzy. But make sure you have money to buy yourself lunch."

"I'm rich, Mister Billy," Suzy said before letting out a big belly laugh, which caused Billy to just shake his head.

Inside the store, Suzy grabbed a large dog biscuit from the pet section before heading to the Sandwich shop near the entrance. In front of her was Josh, wearing a black Ramones shirt and he bobbed his head in excited anticipation of lunch. He ordered his submarine sandwich the same way. Every time the employee behind the counter asked if he wanted another siding or condiment, Josh just kept saying "yes" until his sandwich became a mountain of vegetables. The owner was familiar with this routine and learned to taper Josh's requests. But today there was a new, teenage employee behind the counter who was enjoying making the world's largest sandwich for Josh. Finally, Billy stepped in, nodding to the employee and said, "Josh buddy, that's going be too much" as the employee struggled to wrap it up.

When Suzy herself ordered a full-size sub, Billy was surprised. "Are you gonna be able to eat the whole thing, Suzy?"

"I give half to Lucy and the lady, Mister Billy," Suzy replied, pointing outside as to remind her teacher of her mission.

"Oh, that's sweet, Suzy." He softly patted her on the shoulder.

"Should I buy her a toothbrush Mister Billy. She have brown teeth," Suzy said, her eyebrows coming together from concern.

"If you want, we can go back and get one and some toothpaste." Billy rubbed his chin, feeling somewhat awkward, but since Suzy would be handing off the dental products, he didn't think the lady would be offended.

After the kids bought their sandwiches to take back to school, they strolled around the store to buy one item to take home. Katie bought her mom some Chapstick while Earl got his brother a comb. Suzy grabbed a toothbrush and toothpaste and they all headed for registers. In the checkout line, Suzy remembered to get her dad some bubble gum. Overseeing their purchases, Heather and Billy helped each student count their money.

Once outside of the store, Suzy pushed Justin's chair quickly, eager to give Lucy her snack.

Waiting on the bench, the lady grinned widely as Suzy approached her. "Well, aren't you nice."

Suzy took out her sandwich and gave half of it to the lady, saying, "You and Lucy can share. Does she like sandwiches?"

"Yes, she does sweetheart. What is your name?"

"Suzy. But my Dad calls me Snuzy. And my teacher calls me Miss Suzy. What's your name?

"Alice." She said extending her hand to Suzy.

After shaking her hand, Suzy pulled out her other purchases. "Oh. Here's a toothbrush and toothpaste so after you eat. And you can come to my birthday party. It's July 19th. We have lots of cake."

"Well, thank you. I will do my best to be there."

Suzy put half of the sandwich in her backpack. "Ok, Lucy. We have to go to school. See you later. You be good doggy," Suzy said, and started pushing Justin's wheelchair forward.

About fifty yards down the sidewalk where it comes to an end, Suzy stopped and turned back to Billy.

"Mister Billy. My feet hurt. Can I sit in Justin's chair with him and you push us?"

"Suzy, you won't fit in there. The van is only like 50 more feet. You can make it."

"Okay," she exhaled, "but I'm tired. I need to rest."

"You got this, girl."

High School Football on Friday nights under the lights is a tradition in the South on par with sweetened iced tea and buttered grits. The West End High School stadium has a capacity of 3,500 seats, triple the number of students that attend, but rarely will one find an empty seat. In fact, the games are so popular that many fans end up standing along the fence that encircles the stadium.

The seven o'clock game time came with the first dip of air temperature at night, making it feel like autumn and the perfect kickoff for football season. The hometown was eager for the rematch versus Crossville High, the team that defeated them on the run to last year's state playoffs.

Suzy's Brother Daniel and his girlfriend Charlotte escorted Suzy early to the stadium and grabbed front row seats. Charlotte wore Daniel's letter jacket that revealed numerous wrestling title emblems. While moving up this year to the more competitive hundred and fifty pound weight division for his junior season, he still aspired to finally make it to State and trained all summer long. While Suzy resembled her Dad with her fair skin, Daniel's looked more like his mother with dark hair and tan complexion. Because of his tight, compact frame, thick neck and square jaw, his friends nicknamed him Pit bull.

The game entertained all in attendance and provided the desired drama with the lead changing four times in the first half. But as usual, Suzy was oblivious to what was happening between the hash marks and instead sat mesmerized by the cheer squad in front of her. While she tried to mimic their arm moves, she was almost always off a beat and mumbled most of the cheers as she struggled to keep up. Suzy's eyes would go completely wide when the Squad performed their gymnastic stunts like the back-tuck basket; and her whole body would freeze up in nervousness when they did the dangerous two and half high pyramid. It was crystal clear in Suzy's mind: the crowd showed up to watch the cheer squad and the football team was just background singers.

Emery Lane, the star of the football team, opened the second half by returning the kickoff ninety yards for a touchdown, causing a huge eruption from the sidelines among the home crowd. Daniel and Charlotte leapt to their feet, high fiving other students behind them. On the sidelines, the cheerleaders jumped spontaneously in joy and Suzy found herself caught up in the emotion, leaping up out of her seat and kicking high into the sky above.

Distracted by all the celebration, Suzy hadn't noticed Max, a tall, skinny freshman walking her way with a coke and hot dog in his hand. Her kick caught his front arm, knocking the ice-cold coke into his chest and drenching him.

"Look out you stupid, retard!" Max screamed; his eyebrows furrowed.

Daniel had just turned around and heard the insult. Veins bulging in his neck, he thrust himself in front of Suzy, and grabbed a fistful of Max's shirt, shouting, "Did you just call my sister a retard?"

Instantly Max's face went pale, as he stammered, "Uh, I'm, I'm, sorry."

Suzy put her arms around Daniel to keep him from swinging and tried to push him to the side. Now it was her eyebrows that furrowed, and she yelled at Max, "I'm not a retard. I have Down Syndrome. It's a genetic thing. You not understand."

"I'm really sorry. Please tell your brother not to kill me," Max said, taking a step back.

Letting go of her grip, she pointed her index finger at Daniel and said, "Brother, be good. Don't kill him."

Daniel didn't respond and Max took this as his chance to escape, running back towards the concessions. Charlotte grabbed Daniel by an arm to bring him back to their seat on the bleachers. The nearby crowd that witnessed the confrontation were split on the outcome, as some had wanted a fight while others were relieved the conflict had ended.

Sitting back down, Charlotte rubbed the back of Daniel's neck, trying to get him to relax, but he didn't stop clenching his jaw until the fourth quarter. Suzy, however, didn't miss a beat as she quickly got over the confrontation and went right back to watching the cheer show, attempting to keep her arms in sync to the rhythm of the pom poms.

Chapter 3

The following Tuesday before the end of the school day, the Magnificent Seven watched an inspirational video Billy Martin put on the big screen in his classroom, featuring a disabled teenager who overcame several physical obstacles to get into the Special Olympics.

Heather knocked on the classroom door with some paperwork from the Principal's office for him to sign so Billy stepped right outside so the kids would not be distracted, but kept the door cracked so he still could keep an eye on them.

Wanting to scare Billy when he came back inside, Suzy snuck over to the wall, easing up to the doorway and waited.

While he signed the documents, Heather asked, "By the way, did you ever talk to the Cheer Coach about Suzy joining the team?"

"Yes. I didn't even want to talk to you about it because it got me so infuriated. I asked her after school one day and she just brushed me off, basically telling me they didn't have room on their 'championship squad' for a Downs kid," Billy said, throwing up quotation marks even though that wasn't what Sherry had said.

"Are you serious?" Heather asked, cocking her head to the side.

"Yeah, it's like she wouldn't even consider it. I actually wanted to go off and give her a piece of my mind," he said clasping his hands after signing the paperwork.

"Oh man, that's a bummer. It would be such a kick to see her out there."

"I know, right?" Billy finished, just as the final school bell rang.

Heather sighed and shook her head. "Oh well, I gotta get these up to the office. I'll see you tomorrow."

When Billy entered the room, Suzy didn't burst at him as planned. Instead she just stood there, staring at the floor.

His eyes went wide because she actually did frighten him. He was now worried that she heard his conversation with Heather.

"Hey Suzy, were you trying to scare me, buddy? You always get me." Billy tried to play it off.

When Suzy didn't respond, but kept her gaze down, Billy put his hand on her shoulder and said to all the kids, "Come on guys, get your backpacks and let's get to the bus."

On the way to the bus, Billy kept checking to see if Suzy had changed her demeanor. Her face remained expressionless, leaving him unsure of what to say.

After the kids loaded on the bus, and while the Bus driver helped Justin with his wheelchair through the back-door Handicap ramp, Billy walked up inside and said, "Hey, I really look forward to seeing all of y'all tomorrow." There was a murmuring of goodbyes, but Billy caught

Suzy just staring to the side out the bus window. He walked slowly back down the bus steps, knowing intuitively that Suzy had heard his talk with Heather.

Henry the bus driver knew something was amiss, too. Catching glances of her in his rearview mirror during his route, it was obvious to him that something troubled the usually vibrant Miss Suzy.

Brian kept checking his watch, trying to finish up an email before he needed to head to the bus stop to meet his daughter. His insurance company allowed him to work from home as an underwriter, giving him a flexible schedule and enabling him to be around when Suzy got home from school.

Jogging out to the street corner, Brian arrived just as the bus pulled up. When the door opened, he put his hand out to help Suzy down the steps. Once she was on the pavement, the driver waved Brian over closer to him. "Hey, I think something is wrong with Suzy. She didn't even say hi or bye to me."

"Thanks for the heads up, Henry," Brian said, wondering if she didn't feel well.

Already walking toward the house without her dad, Suzy held her head low as Brian caught up and grabbed her by the hand.

He waited to see if Suzy would share with him what was wrong, but she remained silent. Entering the living room, Brian helped take off her backpack and said, "Hey Booga, is there anything wrong."

Suzy's face went immediately deep red as she plunged herself into Dad's arms. Sobbing loudly, she said something into his shirt, but Brian knew it would take a while before she calmed down enough so he would be able to understand her. When completely distraught, many times she would try to explain, but between gasping for air and crying, she would not be able to articulate what was wrong.

His heart ached as he knew he could do nothing but hold his sweet daughter right now, trying to console her.

After a few minutes, he said, "It's okay, Booga. Daddy's here. I'm gonna take care of you," guiding her to sit on the sofa with him.

Right then, Maria walked through the front door, holding a bag of groceries. She immediately put them down on the floor and hurried over to Suzy, "What's wrong with mi bebe?" she asked in her Puerto Rican accent.

Retrieving some Kleenex from the coffee table, Brian held a tissue on Suzy's nose, letting her blow a couple of times until she began to breathe normally again. She still babbled incoherently, and her parents thought she was saying something about not being able to sit in a chair.

While Brian continued to try to comfort her, Maria picked up the bag of groceries and went to the kitchen. She pulled out her cell phone and dialed Billy Martin who picked up after two rings.

"Hey Billy, Suzy came home and is hysterical," Maria whispered quickly. "She's crying and we can't figure out what's wrong. She keeps saying something about a chair. Did something happen at school?"

"Oh my gosh, Maria. I'm so sorry. Let me try to catch you up to speed." Brian relayed to Maria about Suzy's dream to be a cheerleader, how he approached the coach, but they didn't have any openings and how Suzy overheard the conversation with Heather that she couldn't join the team.

"Don't worry, Billy. It's not your fault. You know how much we appreciate you and are so glad you have been Suzy's teacher."

"Thank you. I was so bummed when I saw her go silent. I had a bad feeling she heard us talking."

"It's okay. Now we know what's going on. I'm going to go talk to her. Have a good day."

"You, too. Goodbye."

Daniel came home from school and when he entered the living room, he wasn't sure what to think or say when he saw his sister crying so he immediately went to the kitchen. He grabbed a Gatorade out of the fridge and whispered to his mom just as she got off the phone, "What's wrong with Suzy?"

"She wants to be a cheerleader, but the coach said they don't have any room. Let's try to encourage her," Maria said softly, waving for him to follow her. Daniel nodded and they headed back into the living room.

Suzy had stopped crying and was now leaning against her dad, grabbing his earlobe, a routine she developed when she was sad.

While Daniel sat down next to his sister, Maria knelt on the floor in front of Suzy and said, "Teacher told me you want to be on the cheer team, but they're already full. But you'll always be our cheerleader hija. You remember when Dad was worried about his job and you told him it would be ok? Remember when I was sad when Abuela was sick and you hugged me, telling me not to cry? You are the best cheerleader in the world."

"But I wanna be cheerleader for football team," Suzy shared. "Now my dream not come true."

"Well, we can pray about it. God hears you," Brian added, pulling her closer to him. "And your Mama's right. Do you know what cheers me up? Your big smile. And people tell me all the time how much they love the way you laugh and how it makes them feel good. You are like a cheerleader for the whole world."

"Hey Chiquita," Daniel said, nudging her with his arm. Chiquita was Daniel's nickname for her since they were in elementary school.

"Quien es el luchador mejor en todo el mundo?" Daniel asked her 'who is the greatest wrestler in the world' in Spanish.

"Your arms are number one. Your legs are number one," Suzy said in a Spanish accent. She had every line memorized from the cult classic film Nacho Libre.

"That's right. And you Chiquita are my number one Cheerleader. I need you screaming for me this year. I can't win without you."

Suzy released her Dad's earlobe, leaning over to her brother and hugging him.

"Si, mi luchador. Siempre," Suzy answered back in Spanish, 'yes, my wrestler. Always'. "Ok. Can I watch TV now?" Suzy said, a clear sign her pain was subsiding.

"Yes, I am gonna get dinner started," Maria said, heading back into the kitchen.

Brian needed to complete some work in his office and contemplated going to finish up before dinner.

Every veteran parent will tell another parent who has young kids that they need to enjoy it while they can because it all goes by so fast. But the new parents never really understand that truth until they actually experience the brevity of time for themselves. Brian had heard it himself, but here he sat, not knowing how his little girl was already in her last year of High School. So, Brian decided the work could wait. Right then, he just wanted to stay on the couch and hold his daughter.

Chapter 4

The high-heeled shoes echoed off the hard wood floors as Sherry paced back and forth beside the countertop of the local bagel shop. Scrolling thru her planner on her phone, Sherry attempted to resolve a scheduling conflict that had come up with the cheer team. Somehow, they were supposed to be at a fund raiser next Friday for the animal shelter at five o'clock for an hour and half appearance, but also be at an Away game by seven PM. She couldn't remember how this even happened and if it was her fault.

"Cheese bagel to go," the college age kid with a nose ring announced. The dark bags under his eyes revealed he was too exhausted to remember who had ordered it.

Sherry knew her order should be ready, but when the other three customers didn't respond, she sensed there must be a mistake.

"I ordered a cheese and spinach bagel. Did you mean that?" She asked, approaching the cashier and putting her phone in her purse.

"No cheese and spinach bagel orders. Just a cheese bagel."

Sherry turned hurriedly to the other customers, "Did y'all order a cheese bagel?", but everyone shook their heads no.

"Ok, well that is not mine. And I was here first. So where is my cheese and spinach bagel?"

Letting out a puff of air, he looked backed at the other employee behind him who was within earshot for help. "Well, we are actually out of cheese and spinach bagels."

"Then why did you even take my order?" Sherry said, placing her hand on her chin.

The cashier looked over his shoulder again at his co-worker who was wrapping up a burrito and keeping his focus down and offering no assistance. Turning back to Sherry, he said, "Uh, yeah, sorry, but we just figured that out."

"You clearly don't have it figured out. It's not freaking rocket science," Sherry blurted out. She wanted to say more but turned away and marched out to her car.

Hurrying into her car and slamming the door shut, Sherry looked in the rearview mirror to put on some lipstick. She glimpsed at her watch before resuming her stare into the mirror. She let out a big sigh, irritated that she had just lost her cool and insulted the kid. But she didn't even have time to go back in the shop to apologize as she needed to leave now to attend a meeting with the Principal before school started.

After starting up her car, Sherry texted Dave: "Can you please bring me something to eat. Sandwich shop screwed up my order. Anything. Bread and water is good. Love U."

Immediately Dave texted her back: "Sure thing. I'll put it in a bag in the lounge fridge."

The Principal Jim Stanley was waiting for Sherry to arrive as he was always the first person on campus. Hired only seven years ago, Stanley turned West End into one of the best schools academically in North Georgia while also helping to rejuvenate the athletics program. After discussing her current scheduling conflict, Jim agreed to call the Animal Shelter and see if they could work on another date or time if Sherry did him a favor. West End High School was hosting a special preseason wrestling event in a few weeks, featuring several top-notch programs. Jim wanted to showcase West End's new facilities, but also create an exciting atmosphere that would bring more tournaments like this back to his school. He wanted both the marching band and the cheerleaders there to make the future Saturday event a huge success. After checking her schedule, Sherry agreed to bring the girls who were available before she hurried off to her classroom.

The rest of the day felt like an immense grind for her. Teaching History to kids is rarely easy, especially High School students. The students rarely seem to see the importance or the relevance so keeping them engaged is always a challenge. At the end of the last period, Sherry was relaying the sacrifices made by abolitionists in England when two senior students in the back of the class began talking just above a whisper to each other.

"Excuse me, gentlemen," she stated. Immediately they knew she was addressing them.

Sherry pursed her lips. "I'm sure you all know the phrase 'those who do not know History are doomed to repeat it'. Well, for some of you that is literally going to happen. I mean, you are going to end up repeating this same History class. Simply because you couldn't pay attention."

To her relief, the final school bell rang. Sherry proceeded to sit down at her desk and the two boys avoided her gaze as they rushed out of the room. Fortunately for them, she didn't have the energy to keep them after class for further reprimanding. Staring blankly at the back wall of her classroom, Sherry's stomach grumbled, reminding her the only thing she consumed all day was some coffee and half a banana that another teacher shared. She got up and scurried down to the teachers' lounge to discover that Dave, true to his words, left her a brown paper bag with a sandwich in it. With a black marker, He labeled the bag, THE Sherry Tinsdale.

She finished eating half the ham and cheese sandwich in the hallway before making it back to her empty classroom, but as she attempted to finish the second half at her desk, her cell phone interrupted the meal.

Chad Casper's name appeared on her screen and Sherry answered before it buzzed again.

Twenty-nine years old, Chad was Sherry's younger brother by only three years. He lived in Alabama with his wife, Gina, and their 3-year old daughter.

"Well hello, Stranger. Long time," she said, leaning back in her chair and put her feet on the desk.

"Hey sis. How's everything?" he asked in his Southern accent.

"Oh goodness. Just busy as a bee. I got Cheer practice in thirty minutes. What's new with you and the fam?"

He let out a big breath. "Man, I have been going thru it. But I think everything is gonna work out now."

Sherry put her feet back on the floor and leaned on to the desk with both elbows. "What's been going on, Chad?"

"Well, that's why I haven't called you for a while." Just over five months to be exact since they last talked.

"I wasn't sure what to think. I had some weird splotches on the back of my neck that Gina noticed. Finally got them checked out and it was skin cancer. Basal cell carcinoma, which isn't too bad. They did what they call an excisional surgery about two weeks ago and the Doc thinks I should be fine. We won't know for sure for another few weeks."

"Jeez, Chad. I wish I had known," Sherry said, rubbing her forehead.

"Since I wasn't sure of the prognosis, I just decided to wait until I knew more before I worried you. But like I said, I feel good that everything is going to work out now. I know it sounds cliché but this whole ordeal was a wakeup call. I had just fallen into the trap. You know, allowing each day to blur into the next. Work, eat, sleep, rinse, repeat. But this cancer scare put a fire under my butt. I want to try to live each day to the fullest, to really be there for my family and help others where I can. I just want to be present."

"Hmmm…." Sherry muttered softly, contemplating what he just said.

"And I'm really sorry for not calling you earlier, but at least now I could actually let you know what I know."

"Don't worry about it, I totally understand. Your words actually resonated with me about trying to be present." She paused, closing her eyes. "I, uh, I've been in a bad rut myself." A lump formed in her throat, causing her to stop talking.

Because she was silent, Chad said, "Well sis, I know you are busy, but I wanted to tell you that I love you and you mean the world to me."

"I love you, too, Chad. Let's talk soon, ok?" she said, her voice quivering as she fought back tears.

"Okay, bye." Click.

Laying the phone down, Sherry collapsed into her folded arms on the desk. Her battle to stay composed was over. In the privacy of her empty room, the damn of pent up emotions finally ruptured, and a flood of tears burst forth.

After a few minutes she stopped crying and pulled a Kleenex from inside her desk drawer, rubbing her wet nose and wiping the tears off her face.

Grateful for her unexpected conversation with Chad, Sherry recognized it could not have come at a better time. Surprised at how refreshed she felt after this cathartic release, Sherry took a deep breath as she reflected on what Chad said, "I want to be present", echoing in her thoughts.

For the past six months, discouragement had reigned, leaving her emotionally fatigued and mentally exhausted.

My pain has shackled me for way too long and today has to be the day it stops, she thought. *This is the time to shake off the past and move on. Like Chad, I need to be resolved to live each day as best as I can.*

Now she saw that she would make that choice to start to live again. Thinking of all the people in her life, she wanted nothing more than to share with them that Sherry Tinsdale was back.

Eagerly grabbing her phone, she texted Dave: "Need to talk tonight. Good stuff. Love you."

Putting her phone in her purse, Sherry walked quickly out to meet her cheer squad at the football stadium. The girls were already practicing on the track beside the field. As Sherry approached them, she put on her sunglasses to conceal she had been weeping.

"Girls, gather in because I need to talk. In three weeks, there is a huge wrestling tournament here in the gym and the Principal wants us to be there. It's at noon on a Saturday so this is not compulsory, but you'd be doing me a big favor if you can come. Please let me know by next Friday if you can attend."

"Now on to something more personal. Some of you guys may not know that I have been going through some serious personal issues," Sherry said, taking a breath to gather herself before continuing. "First of all, since then, I haven't been myself. And I know I must not have been too pleasant to even be around at times."

Amanda glanced over to Assistant Coach Melissa, wondering if she disclosed to Sherry that Amanda was unhappy about the way things were on the team. Melissa raised her eyebrows to her, trying to signal that this was news to her as well and had kept their conversation confidential.

Sherry put her hands together in front of her before continuing. "I am sorry for not making this what it should be for y'all. This should be fun. Yes, we need to work hard and try our best, but these should be some of the best days of your lives. Today feels like a break thru for me, that I can put my own pain to the side at least and try to live in the now. So I hope I can be a better coach for you guys moving forward."

Amanda smiled over to Melissa, relieved to see and hear her coach acknowledge she was making some positive changes.

"And before I forget, thank you guys for all your hard work and dedication," Sherry continued. She then pointed over to the end zone, saying, "Today, I want us to focus more on our pyramid skills. Let's move over to the grass and I'm going to come over and help spot."

The tension on the team that had been building seemed to be instantly released. With their coach now relaxed, the team experienced a great practice, and the girls appeared to truly enjoy themselves for the first time in ages.

When Sherry arrived home, she could smell steak grilling on the deck. Walking through the house and dropping her purse on the kitchen table, she pushed the sliding glass door open to find Dave flipping a couple of T-bones.

Seeing her out of the corner of his eye, he turned around smiling, "Hope you're hungry."

She wanted to tell him everything that happened after school, but her emotions caused her to just push herself into her husband, wrapping her arms around him. Another flood of tears unloaded from deep within her as she sobbed into his chest.

Dave went silent for a few minutes before saying, "Honey, is everything ok? I thought you had some good news?"

Sherry sniffed before saying, "Yes. I want to share what happened today. Are the steaks done?"

"Yes, let me just turn off the grill and flip them one more time," he said before they moved over to the patio table and sat down.

Sherry grabbed his hand, sharing the story of her brother's phone call and how it ended up moving her to the core.

"Dave, I was just wanting to say how much I appreciate you. I know you have been trying your hardest to help me. I feel like we lost a lot of time and I never again want to feel distant from you. I need you to forgive me."

Dave looked into her eyes, smiling to hear his wife's heart was finally healing. "Sweetie, there is nothing to forgive. Everybody grieves differently."

She reached over and kissed him passionately. After a minute, she stood up, grabbing his hand and leading him inside. The steaks would have to wait.

Chapter 5

Saturday morning, Brian finished up some work in his office while Suzy ate cereal and watched her favorite cartoon, the illustrious Sponge Bob Square Pants. With Maria working as an on-call nurse at a local medical clinic and Daniel at wrestling practice, Brian planned to devote the rest of the morning to some quality time with Suzy.

"So does Daddy's girl want to go downtown and hang out?" Brian asked, standing in front of her and trying to get her attention.

"Dad, I'm watching Sponge Bob," Suzy said, annoyed that he blocked the view of the TV.

"I think you have all the episodes memorized. Let's go outside and stretch the legs," Brian said, moving toward the front door and hoping she would motivate.

"No want," Suzy said sternly, nodding her head side to side.

"Come on, we'll have fun," Brian said, trying to encourage her and extending his hand toward her.

"Nnnnn," she grunted.

The more Suzy didn't want to do something, the shorter her answers became. Brian thought for years that Suzy's stubbornness was just one of her personality traits before he found out that it was common among Down Syndrome children.

"Well, what if I let you drive?" Brian stated, knowing it would shock her.

Suzy's eyes lit up as her demeanor and tone completely switched. "I can drive? I'm a big girl!"

"That's right. You are a big girl. And today is the big day that you get to drive."

Grabbing the remote, she turned the TV off and put her shoes on as fast as she could.

"Whoa, I have not seen you move that fast since we went to get frozen yogurt," Brian quipped.

For the past two years, she told her dad repeatedly she wanted to drive and to get her own car. He knew she did not have the skill set to drive safely, but this morning he had an idea.

The plan was simple. With Suzy sitting in his lap, Brian would let her control the steering wheel while he controlled the brakes and gas. Her short legs could not reach the pedals anyway and Brian's long arms allowed him to keep a hand on the wheel. Just in case.

After sitting down in the black 2003 Chevy Suburban driver's seat, Brian pushed the seat back as far it would go. Suzy climbed in and squeezed between the wheel and Brian. After warming up the engine, Brian put the vehicle into drive gear, and they started down their street.

The small subdivision they lived in held just over fifty homes, all built in the late Eighties. Each track home's design essentially repeated itself every fifth house and most homes sat on almost an acre of land.

Pointing ahead, Brian said, "Now just steer straight Suzy like you're playing a video game."

"Ima get my own car," she said, excitedly.

"Yeah, calm your jets down on that one, buddy. Let's see if you can make it out of the neighborhood without running over a garbage can."

After they had driven about fifty yards, they saw Mr. Klein looking down and walking out to his mailbox.

"Hit the horn, Suzy," Brian said, and she pushed down, startling Mr. Klein and causing him to look up. When he saw Suzy driving, his jaw fell open.

"Hey Mr. Klein! Look at me. I'm driving," Suzy shouted out the window.

Not seeing Brian actually steering the vehicle, he stood in disbelief and waved slowly at her.

"Okay, Miss Snuzy. You just hit a top speed of seven miles per hour!" Brian informed her.

"Oh yeah!" Suzy exclaimed proudly.

"At this stop sign coming up, I want you to turn right. We'll do a lap around the old hood."

Suzy turned gradually and Brian drove slower as there were some cars parked along the oncoming street.

"Don't hit these cars or Daddy is gonna be in big trouble."

"I got this, Dad," she said, turning back to look at him.

"Keep your eyes on the road and grip the wheel with two hands. Now, I think we need some music. James Brown work for you?"

Letting out a sigh and rolling her eyes, she looked back toward the road and replied, "Not again, Dad."

"I'm not gonna dance, Suz," he promised and pushed in a CD. "Yes, now we are rolling with Maceo, Bootsy and the God Father of Soul."

"What in the world?" Suzy asked, perplexed by the musical reference.

"Don't worry about it. You just enjoy driving to the power of funk."

"Dad, you're weird," Suzy said in a deep voice, knowing it would make his Dad laugh. Which it did.

Making the circle around the neighborhood unscathed, Brian asked Suzy, "You wanna keep going?"

Shaking her head enthusiastically, she answered, "Yes, this is awesome. Can we drive to Mama's work?"

"Definitely no. That's too far anyway, Snuzy. And I'm not sure your Mom needs to know about this little outing."

"Why not?" Suzy asked, turning her head back again toward Brian.

"I'll be asking the questions around here. And remember, keep your eyes on the road. Up here we are gonna take a left at this next intersection."

After they slowed to a stop, Brian looked both ways before telling her to drive onto a public road. When she completed the turn, Brian hit the gas to the floor, causing the vehicle to leap forward and Suzy screamed.

Brian immediately let off the gas while laughing, "Got ya."

"Dad that scared me. Don't do that," Suzy demanded, forgetting his instructions and turning her head back again.

"Okay, Snuz. I thought you might wanna go fast for a second."

"No. You have tell me first. Can we go to the store and get a coke? I'm thirsty."

"Sure, that sounds good."

Putting on the hazard lights, Brian kept scanning the rearview mirror while they drove fifteen MPH on this double lane country road with no other cars in sight.

It was a perfect day outside, a cool seventy-seven degrees out, and not a cloud to be found. Brian treasured these moments with his daughter. He leaned up, kissed her on the cheek, and could feel the smile on her face. Brian didn't know if Suzy would eventually be able to move out on her own, but he would be content if she never left home.

As they approached the first stop light, they needed to take a right to get to the 7-11.

After coming to a stop at the vacant four way, Brian noticed a car speeding up beside them. Brian reached over and turned down the music as a yellow convertible with the top down eased up beside them at the red light. The brand-new Camaro's engine rumbled loudly over the engine of the Suburban. Leaning his car seat back even more, hiding himself behind the rolled up and darkly tinted back seat window, Brian was confident the Camaro's driver could not see him.

Brian revved the engine loudly with his right foot, trying to announce a challenge to the Camaro. To his delight, he spied the young male driver peering over at them. Brian then noticed him push his sunglasses down to see if his eyes were playing tricks on him or if he really was witnessing a Downs person driving a vehicle.

Brian whispered to Suzy, "Ask him if he wants to race."

Putting on a serious face, Suzy leaned out of the window toward the Camaro, yelling, "Do you wanna piece of me?"

"What?" the driver asked, shaking his head as if in a dream.

"You wanna race?" Suzy gripped the wheel, daring him.

"Pfffttt…You wanna lose?" he said cockily.

The traffic light went green, tires squealed, and a cloud of smoke poured out from underneath the Camaro. In less than five seconds, they could barely see the back of the Camaro.

Brian laughed out loud before releasing the brake. "Oh yeah, Suzy. Turn the wheel, we need to take a right here."

"I thought we were gonna race?" she asked, confused as to why they were still sitting there at the intersection, but cranking the wheel to the right.

"Next time, Snuzy. Next time," Brian said as they pulled into the 7-11 entrance, still chuckling that the other driver had taken the bait.

Climbing out of the Suburban, Suzy headed inside the store while Brian stretched his legs first. Back by the cooler, she reached in and grabbed a plastic bottle of coke, unscrewed the top and started guzzling it while Brian made his way down the aisle towards her.

"Hey, you gotta pay first, Suzy," Brian said, reaching into his jeans pocket for his wallet.

"I don't have any money," she said, letting out a burp.

"I know. That's why you need to wait. Now here's five dollars. You need to practice buying things like they are teaching you at school. And don't burp in public like that."

Suzy marched up to the register as Brian grabbed a Gatorade from the cooler. As he walked up behind her, he saw Suzy toss the five-dollar bill at the clerk and walk away to the front door.

"Suzy!" Brian yelled, getting her attention. "Get back over here."

The clerk just stood there looking at the five dollars.

"You need to wait for your change. Five dollars is too much for a coke."

"But it's a good coke," she said, wiping her mouth with her hand.

"I'm sure it is. Coke is good. But wait for the man to give you your change." Brian smiled at the clerk.

Back outside and getting readjusted into the driver's seat, Brian decided they better head back to the house. No more than five minutes later and about a half mile down the road, he noticed a Sheriff's car approaching in the oncoming lane. The Sheriff reduced his speed, no doubt wondering why the Suburban was cruising so slowly with the hazard lights on.

Holding his breath, Brian let out a big gasp of relief when the Sherriff passed by. But looking in the rearview mirror, he discovered the red and blue emergency lights had been flipped on and the patrol car completing a three-point turn. The Sherriff was now in hot pursuit of the Suburban.

Brian found a grassy knoll to pull over and turn the vehicle off, grabbing his wallet back out of the console.

As the Sherriff walked up to the car, Suzy asked, "Dad, are we in trouble?"

"Just stay calm, Suzy," Brian said, but wondering the same question.

Wearing the traditional Sherriff Brown uniform, but also donning a cowboy hat and mirrored sunglasses, the mustached officer started in with the standard operating procedure.

"Mam, I need to see your license and registration."

"Uh, I have a school ID," Suzy answered, not knowing what registration even meant.

"Mam, that's not gonna cut it. I need you to slowly step out of the vehicle," the serious voice of authority commanded.

"Dad!" Suzy shouted, her body becoming stiff from fear.

"It's okay, Sweetie, you can relax," Brian said, now realizing he knew the Officer. "What's up, Darrel?"

"Don't worry, Suzy. I know you," Darrel said chuckling, removing his glasses. "Do you know me?" The officer's voice changed from stern to friendly as he crouched down beside the window so he was eye level with her.

"You're Tommy dad," she said no recognizing him.

"That's right. You learning how to drive, sweetie?"

"Yes. I'm a big girl," she said, demonstrating her grip on the wheel.

"I see that," he said, standing back up and resting his thumbs on his belt. "But you need to slow down. I saw you guys pass a turtle back there. You always need to remember the goal is to 'arrive alive'."

Brian cackled, but Suzy's forehead scrunched up, puzzled, before she said, "I didn't see a turtle."

"Okay guys, y'all be safe now and we'll see ya at church tomorrow," Darrel said, before heading back to his patrol car.

Suzy turned her head to the side. "Dad, should I ask him if he wants to race?"

"No, we should probably make that your last race of the day," Brian said, relieved that the Sherriff had been a friend from Church.

When the Suburban pulled back in front of their house, they noticed Maria had gotten off work early and was now getting something out of the trunk of her car in the driveway.

As soon as Brian removed the seat belt and opened the car door, Suzy bounded out of his lap, sprinting up to Maria.

"Mama, Mama, I was driving. I am a big girl now!" she said, hopping up and down.

"You were driving?" she asked, her eyes peering over at Brian.

"Yes Mama, we raced around the neighborhood and got pulled over by the police. It was so much fun," she said rapidly before running into the house.

Maria crossed her arms and glared at Brian. "Soooo…what did you guys do?" She asked slowly, looking for an explanation.

"Well, we drove down to Atlanta. Suzy was driving really well so I jumped in the back and took a nap. Next thing I know, I wake up and she's racing some sports car before the cops finally pull us over. But the cop was nice, and just gave us a warning. How was your day?"

By not responding and looking up, Maria's face told Brian his joke had failed, and he had to come clean.

"We just went for a little cruise down the street. I let her sit on my lap. Darrel from Church was in his patrol car and pulled Suzy over to give her the business. It was hilarious."

"I'm gonna slap you, Brian Beckham," Maria said, shaking her head, but now unable to hide a grin.

Even though Maria had been raised in San Juan until she was sixteen, her Puerto Rican accent had a Southern drawl to it now, and she had also picked up some mannerisms along the way like saying the full name of your husband or child when you mean business.

Walking toward the house and not wanting Suzy to hear his next comment, Brian said softly, "Oh, I think we need to get Suzy to a see that Orthopedist again. Her teacher texted me that she is complaining at school about her feet."

"Awww. Mi nina. I wonder if her shoes are not wide enough."

"I looked at them again and they look fine to me. Get that Doctor's number and I can call to get her an appointment. I just hope it's not something serious."

The faculty and student body did not disappoint Principal Stanley when West End held their first ever North Georgia High School Wrestling Tournament. Wrestling was not an immensely popular spectator sport at West End and few people attended the meets. However, this Saturday afternoon the gym looked completely different. The stands were packed with people, the cheerleaders and band were bringing the energy, creating a rousing atmosphere.

Suzy sat front row, with her parents on one side, and her classmate Katie on the other. Katie was new to the wrestling meets as her brother Stephen was only a freshman contestant, while the youngest starter on Varsity, Stephen was still the biggest kid on the team and headed up the heavyweight division.

Ever since Middle School, Suzy liked to play Mama Bear with the other kids and relished the chance to explain to Katie what they would do during the match.

"When your brother wrestles, we need to scream real loud. That's how he'll win, Ok?" Suzy instructed.

"Ok, ok," Katie said, nodding rapidly.

"And when my brother wrestles, we need to scream real loud. Ok?

"Ok, Suzy." Katie stopped nodding as she needed to push her glasses back up her button nose.

Also on the front row and only thirty feet away from The Beckhams, Coach Sherry sat holding hands with her husband Dave as they observed the Cheer squad while the wrestlers took the mat.

The format was somewhat unique, a round robin tournament with the first matchups predetermined among the contestants. Suzy's brother, Daniel, faced last year's State runner up and this year's perennial favorite, Kyle Bloodworth from Cherokee Ridge.

When Daniel and Kyle finally stood across from each other before their match, Suzy exploded out of her seat, thrusting her right leg in the air and yelled, "Get him, Daniel!"

Brian and Maria chuckled. They had seen that high kick and scream a hundred times, but it still made them laugh every time.

Daniel's coach, James Fulmer, a former All-American at Iowa, was almost as enthusiastic as Suzy. He would crawl on the mat on his belly, near his wrestler, screaming instructions and encouragement.

Kyle and Daniel provided an intense match, with Kyle almost pinning Daniel in the first period before he escaped. The points total switched a few times in the second period and Brian had no idea who was winning as he lost count going into the third and final period.

While Daniel started in bottom position in the third period, he escaped and made up his mind to win on a pin. He could never get the right angle until the final twelve seconds of the match when he threw a leg sweep, putting Kyle on his back. While Daniel moved in to force his opponent's shoulders to the mat, Coach Fulmer lay sprawled out and only feet away from interference, screamed his head off, telling Daniel "It's yours for the taking!"

In the blink of an eye, Suzy ran down on to the mat, and lay next to Coach Fulmer, shouting and banging her arms on the mat, "Come on Daniel! Beat him!"

Daniel finally secured the pin, and Suzy launched up off the mat, doing her patented high kick and jumping around like crazy before running over to her parents.

"Daniel pinned him; Daniel pinned him!" She yelled as if they didn't see it for themselves.

Unfortunately, Suzy did not realize the pin came one second after the final buzzer, causing Daniel to lose by a single point.

Brian tried to explain the loss to Suzy, but she would not believe him, pleading to her dad how she had been up close and saw Daniel win. A minute later, the referee held up Kyle's hand in victory, and Suzy was crushed.

Daniel, however, handled the loss better than other defeats, taking solace he came close to winning against a formidable opponent. In fact, he soon found himself laughing hysterically when his parents relayed the phone video of Suzy running up on the mat.

While many others in attendance were also amused by her antics, the Cheer coach was taking notes on the spontaneity and creativity of one Suzy Beckham.

After Monday's cheer practice on the football field, Sherry asked her two captains to stick around for five minutes extra to talk. It was now mid-October with the night air dropping into the forties, so she didn't want to keep them long.

"Hey guys, I wanted to run something by y'all to get your thoughts. This conversation needs to stay between us, though. Can I get your agreement on that," Sherry said, looking at each girl; all nodded in approval.

"So I know we only have four more regular season games left and it does not look like we will go to the playoffs unless we win the last four, which honestly looks doubtful. But I was wondering if you guys would be open to letting this girl from the Special Ed class come over for some practices. If we could get her up to speed on some basic cheers, I think it would be cool if she could share the field with us. But…this is your team. I think it is only fair that you guys make the call."

Tiffany spoke up, "Who is the girl?"

"Suzy Beckham, she has Down Syndrome," Sherry responded.

"Oh heck yeah, Suzy's a riot. She's in my Choir class and calls me her homie," Tiffany laughed.

The Captain Amanda nodded at her best friend Tiff before saying, "Yeah, I've known Suzy since middle school. She is super sweet. I'm for it."

"I'm gonna contact her teacher to see if she can get to some practices this week. He told me it was her big dream," Sherry said.

"That's gonna be rad. We'll take her under our wings, Coach," Amanda added.

"Okay, let's get outta here. It's freezing," Sherry finished before they rushed off to their cars.

The final bell rang Tuesday and Sherry hurried to the busses hoping to find Suzy and her teacher. Finding the small yellow bus, she arrived before the kids began walking towards her. Since he had avoided her since after their last talk, Billy was surprised to see Sherry standing there. Walking next to Suzy, he unconsciously folded his arms defensively across his chest as he neared the bus.

"Hi Suzy, I'm Sherry Tinsdale, the Cheer Coach," Sherry said, smiling and extending her hand.

Suzy took her hand and shook it, unable to speak as she stood face-to-face with one of her heroes.

"Suzy, I saw your amazing high kick at the wrestling meet. Would you like to come to some of our practices and hang out with the girls? They wanna teach you some cheers."

The blank face on Suzy's face along with no reply puzzled Sherry so she looked over to Billy for help.

Billy leaned down to Suzy. "Miss Suzy, this is your dream come true. Are you ready to meet up with the Cheer team?"

Her eyes stretched wide and still unable to speak, Suzy just slowly nodded yes.

"Well, Suzy is usually very loquacious, but you have left her stunned. That's quite an accomplishment," Billy added.

Sherry smiled at Suzy and said, "I'm gonna get your parents number from Billy and call them to work all the details out. Okay?"

Suzy finally cracked a smile and walked up the steps of the bus and Billy turned to Sherry, "I'm so glad you guys are gonna let her come and hang out. She will be a huge treat for you. I promise."

"If we can get her comfortable doing some cheers, I am going to try to let her on the field during an actual game."

"That would be amazing. She will probably have a heart attack." Billy smiled.

"Well, that would be anti-climactic. Let me get her parents contact info so I can put it in my phone," Sherry asked. After typing in the contact info, she rushed off to cheer practice to meet the girls.

Later that same day, Sherry decided to take a slightly longer route home. Driving on a curvy road through a canyon pass, she admired the sun as it dipped down over a nearby mountain ridge, setting the orange and red tree leaves of autumn in a soothing glow. Sherry couldn't remember the last time she took the time to appreciate the simple beauty of her surroundings.

As she pulled into her driveway, she noticed Dale's truck missing so she decided this would be a good time to call Suzy's parents before he got home.

"Hi, is this Maria Beckham? This is Sherry Tinsdale from West End High School," she quickly added so Maria wouldn't think she was a telemarketer.

Walking out to mailbox, Maria stopped in her tracks. "Yes, is everything okay?"

"Oh, everything is fine. I'm the Cheerleading Coach and wanted to see if Suzy would like to attend some practices after school this week."

"She would love that. What time do they end?" Maria asked, speaking quickly as she did when she got excited about something.

"Usually right around when it gets dark. She doesn't have to stay the whole time and come to every practice. Don't tell her yet, but if we can get her up to speed on some of the basics and she feels comfortable, I would like her to join us on the field during a game."

Maria's face beamed. "Awww. Mi hija. She would be in heaven."

"I am sorry, but I couldn't help detect an accent. Are you from Puerto Rico?"

"Yes, very good. I lived in Rincon until I was fifteen. My parents just retired and moved back there. Have you been there?"

"My family used to spend summers in San Juan. My grandparents are Puerto Rican."

"Are you serious? Habla espanol?"

"Un poquito. Yo tengo hambre por mofongos y empanadillas." Sherry relayed that her Spanish was limited and she was hungry for some authentic Puerto Rican dishes.

Maria laughed, "Well, you need to come over and get some of those dishes because you know you ain't gonna find them in Gilmerton, Georgia."

"That's, too, true. We gotta get together and talk island," Sherry said, thrilled to meet someone from Puerto Rico.

"So Sherry, text me those dates and times of practice. We look forward to meeting you, soon. I need to go make some Papas Rellenos right now."

"Papas Rellenos? I'm on my way over," Sherry joked.

Maria chuckled. "Seriously. We will do it. Thank you so much for calling. Suzy is going to have a blast."

Maria went into the house, eager to tell Suzy the news. When she opened the door, Suzy ran toward her and started leaping spastically in front of her.

"Mama, imacheer, imacheer, imacheer!" Suzy said rapidly.

Sitting on the couch, Brian looked at Maria and shrugged his shoulders. "She's been saying that ever since she got off the bus. I could never make out what she's saying."

"Suzy's gonna cheer!" Maria exclaimed and started leaping up and down with her daughter to celebrate.

"What?" Brian perked up.

"I just got off the phone with the Cheer Coach. She wants Suzy to start coming to the practices."

Now Brian jumped up and said, "Hi five Miss Snuzy! That's awesome. You're gonna be the best Cheerleader ever!"

Seeing the look on Suzy's face and her body language, Brian stepped back, knowing the high kick was coming his way. As she finished thrusting her leg up in the air, both Brian and Maria rushed in to embrace their new cheerleader.

Chapter 6

When Sherry walked into her living room that evening, Dave was watching a replay of the 1998 Final Four game between Utah and North Carolina. Even though Dave played basketball at Vanderbilt, his favorite coach of all time remained Carolina's Dean Smith. To prepare himself for the upcoming season, Dave would watch hours of classic matchups, trying to pick up strategies from opposing coaches.

"Man, I don't know why Coach Smith didn't call a time out in the first half. The game was getting away from them in the first 10 minutes. I'm seriously baffled at what he was thinking," Dave said, patting the couch seat for Sherry to join him.

"Well, honey, even the great ones make mistakes," Sherry said, glancing down at her cell phone in her hand.

Dave leaned over and kissed Sherry on the cheek before asking, "How was your day?"

"Pretty good. But it's been over a week of having practices with Suzy and she's not actually catching on like I hoped. I mean, at first she was kind of timid. Just standing around a lot looking at the girls because she was just in awe of them. But then she warmed up, finally following some of the instruction from Amanda. It was super funny one day because they were teasing her and told Suzy she was going to be on the top of the pyramid. You should have seen her eyes." Sherry chuckled.

"I'd be scared to get up there, too." Dave admitted.

"That's what Suzy said. She goes, 'no way, that's too high for me'. But when the girls said they were just kidding, she busted up laughing. She really has this infectious laugh."

"So do all the girls seem to like having her around?"

"Oh yeah, all the girls love her. And they've been taking extra time with her." Sherry stopped and let out a big breath of air. "The problem is she's always like a half beat behind on the cheers and can't seem to memorize them. She always just kind of mutters them. I wanted to get her into a game, but I'm worried she might distract some on the team from being in sync."

Dave raised his hand, pointing his index upward. "Well, I have an idea."

"Is this from all your years of cheerleading?" Sherry said smiling and put her arm around him.

"Just get your pen and pad out. You need to create 'special' plays for her. Things that she doesn't have to be in step with the others. Like that thing y'all do, where the girls line up across from each other and form a tunnel with their pom poms. Have Suzy run thru the middle of them, and explode out at the end."

"That's actually a great idea. She can run thru and showcase that high kick. She loves doing that. Literally every five minutes," Sherry said, laughing.

"Give her the megaphone. Have her off to the side and saying simple things like, "Go Wildcats!""

"I like it. I am going to ask the girls what else they think we can do. Wow, you have come up with a good game plan, Dave. Maybe you should consider going into coaching?"

"That's cute. When you walk into The Dave Tinsdale Auditorium one day, I think you will remember this little conversation." He spread his arms wide, emphasizing the vastness of the stadium in his name.

"Oh, don't forget the statue of you in front to greet all your adoring fans! Right?" Sherry added mockingly.

Dave put his hand on his chin as if he had to ponder the question more deeply. "You know, it wouldn't really feel right unless it was at least a twenty-foot statue of me shooting a three pointer, would it?"

Sherry rolled her eyes at his dream and then quipped, "Maybe you should start with some small goals. Like finishing a season with a winning record."

Her last comment made Dave laugh out loud. "Now that was just mean. And I will not be sharing with the team what you said about us."

"Well, while you think up your new winning strategy, I got to go to the ladies' room. Can we watch the Travel Channel when I come back?" Sherry stood up and began walking away.

"Sure. That sounds good. I don't like the ending to this game anyway." Dave grabbed the remote to change channels.

On her way down the hallway, it occurred to Sherry that she might be late for her period. She tried going back over the exact dates in her head, now guessing she was around seven days late. Her mind began to race and once inside the bathroom, she rifled through the vanity until she found a pregnancy test. Ripping the packaging off with her teeth and tossing the box in the trash, she sat down and followed the simple instructions she knew by heart.

Now biting her thumb nail as she waited for the results, she stood back up, looking into the mirror on the door and taking deep breaths trying to calm her nerves. Starting to feel flush and claustrophobic, she grabbed the test and walked back out to the living room.

As she neared the couch, she stopped, looking down for the results. Dave turned to see her standing there, holding a short, plastic pink stick.

"Is that a….? He didn't finish the sentence, jumping up from the couch to come stand by her. Placing his hand gently on her arm, he stammered, "I, uh, didn't even know you were late."

Nodding yes, Sherry bit her lip softly while Dave stood frozen, waiting for the answer. Finally, she let out a breath, releasing her bottom lip as she exhaled and gave way to a smile. "It's positive."

Dave threw his arms around her, whispering in her ear, "I told you it would happen again."

Immediately he regretted his word choice, realizing that while he was correct about her getting pregnant again, there was also another chance Sherry would again end up devastated. When he pulled back, her smile was gone. With her gaze on the floor, Dave sensed all the mixed emotions stirring inside his wife. Grabbing her by the hand, he led her over to the couch, hoping he would find the right words to encourage her.

"Sherry, we need to remember that everything we go through is ultimately working for the good. Even the bad times we face. God is gonna carry us thru, I promise. Right now, I understand why you may be apprehensive, so I want to pray."

Keeping her eyes down, Sherry felt awkward and a tinge of guilt for not talking to God for so long. And especially now since the only reason she was praying is because she wanted help. At this point, she was unsure if God would listen to her anyway.

Dave bowed his head. "Heavenly Father, thank you for my wife and bringing us together. I come before you to ask that you please protect Sherry and this child in her womb. And please help us not to worry about what tomorrow may bring. Amen."

Sherry stayed silent but nodded in agreement. While the seeds of doubt remained planted deep within her, she desperately wanted to believe there was reason for hope and that she might finally have her baby.

Tired from the one-hour long visit to the Orthopedic Surgeon and the two-hour roundtrip drive, Suzy predictably fell asleep in the car on the way back home. Somehow, she instinctively woke up within half a mile of her school. Even though the school day just ended, Suzy still wanted to go to cheerleading practice, not really comprehending what the doctor told them earlier. It was a lot to digest and Maria wanted to speak with Sherry anyway, so she agreed to take her to practice.

Walking up to the grass next to the end zone of the stadium where the girls practiced, Suzy began running over to the team. Maria was going to stop her but decided against it and let her just keep going. Seeing Sherry leaning up against the chain link fence analyzing her team, Maria waved at Coach before approaching her.

"Hi Coach. I'm sorry, but I kinda have some bad news. I don't know if you noticed that Suzy's feet have been really bothering her after practice."

"Actually, I thought she was just tired and would sit down. What's going on?"

"Well, she has really bad bunions. Her feet are actually kind of deformed if you were to see her barefoot. I just went back to an Orthopedic Surgeon and we are going to try some new orthotics, but he is recommending surgery," Maria said, her eyes drifting out to where her daughter stood.

Sherry shook her head in disappointment at the news. "Aw man, how long would she be out?"

"That's the hard part. She would be in a boot cast for at least a few weeks, but he said full recovery could take up to a full year. It's so disappointing because the cheerleading was a dream come true for her. She talks about it nonstop at home."

Sherry looked at Maria in the eyes. "Oh, we have loved having her. Your daughter is a real sweetheart."

"Thanks for saying that. Now I need to go talk about it with my husband Brian. Surgery at this point would basically ruin her senior year. She has a special dance in two weeks that she was looking forward to. Maybe the new orthotics will make a difference, but the doctor wasn't sounding so confident they would really help."

"We have come up with some specific cheers for Suzy where she wouldn't have to be on her feet all game long," Sherry offered.

"Okay, we'll have to play it by ear. I also wanted to thank you and all the girls for letting Suzy participate and making her feel so important."

"You do know you can pay me in empanadas, right?" Sherry said, smiling.

"Amiga, we will make dinner happen. I promise you that." Maria then waved and yelled at Suzy to come over.

"Suzy, we need to get you home and off your feet until you get better," Maria said, caressing Suzy's cheek.

"But Mama, I can do it." Suzy pleaded.

"We know you can do it, hija. But you heard the doctor today. And you keep complaining about your feet hurting," Maria said with her hands on her hips, trying to stand firm.

"Please let me stay, Mama. I just watch, ok? Please, please, please?" Suzy continued to beg.

Maria stood no chance against Suzy's puppy dog eyes.

"Ok, but just watch. I'm gonna have dad pick you up. And no driving this time, ok?" Maria joked, but saw Sherry's eyes get big, wondering if Suzy actually drove.

"Don't worry, Sherry. My husband just lets Suzy ride between his legs and steer while they go super slow," Maria said, walking backwards and toward her car now. I'll keep you posted on the feet."

"Have a good day," Sherry said as she and Suzy walked over to the grass area near the team. Suzy sat down cross-legged, twirling her pigtails and watching the girls practice a new pyramid formation. Sherry stood and looked down at Suzy, now questioning whether she would ever get to cheer during a game.

The long car drive and the stress of the orthopedic appointment earlier left Maria feeling exhausted so instead of cooking dinner she ordered a pizza for the four of them. Around the dinner table, Maria relayed what the Doctor had said about Suzy's bunions and the options they faced. Brian agreed with Maria that Suzy could go to practice to watch, but not to participate. The surgery recommendation took him by surprise and somewhat dampened the good news he wanted to share.

"Well, on a positive note, I've been given a great opportunity from Corporate today," Brian started now that everyone had started eating.

"What's that, Sweetie?" Maria smiled, eager to hear the reason for his excitement.

He clasped his hands together in front of himself as if he was praying the news would be welcomed. "They have offered me the Head Underwriting position in Atlanta. My salary will be almost three times what I make now. But I need to let them know by next Friday."

Maria's smile went flat. "But we moved here to get away from the big city."

"Yes, but this is a whole different kind of opportunity. The Head Underwriter doesn't retire every year. Who knows when this same kind of op would come up for me. You were the one who wanted to stay in the city. I thought you would be happy."

"I was reluctant at first, but now I like it. I am content here. Couldn't you do this job from home, too?

"No. I have to be in the office. But with this kind of salary, I might actually be able to retire one day," Brian said, trying to focus on the upside of taking the job.

Daniel remained silent, keeping his stare down and his mother sensed his concern.

Maria countered. "It will be tough on the kids. They basically have to start new at the end of their High School years."

"I know, I have thought of that. Maybe I could move down to Atlanta, rent a place and come up here on weekends," Brian offered.

"For two freaking years?" Maria said, getting louder. The Latin fire was beginning to kindle.

"I don't know. I'm trying to think of ideas of how to make this work. If we go to the city, Suzy could get the surgery and we can afford to have you stay home with her while she heals up. I could even pay for a private, Christian school for Daniel to go to."

"I like my school," Daniel finally said, avoiding eye contact.

"But you would get an even better education, at say, Mount Moriah," Brian added, looking at his son and trying to get him to see the positives.

"What about Charlotte?" Daniel asked, thinking of his girlfriend for the last two years.

"Come on…Do you think you're going to actually marry this girl?" Brian rolled his eyes.

Daniel reared up quickly and bolted for the door.

"Son, I'm sorry. I'm just trying to be pragmatic here…," Brian yelled right before the front door slammed.

"Stupid, why did you say that to him?" Maria's eyebrows narrowed as she glared at him. Before he could answer, Maria stood up and scampered off to the bedroom and Brian heard yet another door slam.

Planting his elbows on the table, he rested his face on his two fists. He let out a big sigh before Suzy said, "Dad, I still wanna be a cheerleader."

Brian reached over and put one of his hands on top of hers, but averted looking at her. "I know sweetie. But we have a lot going on right now."

Sitting there silently, she couldn't comprehend the complexity of career life and family decisions like the one her parents faced. But she did understand there wasn't peace in her house and she no longer felt like eating.

Brian sat there staring at the closed pizza box before him. He had hoped to engage in a dialogue tonight with his family and pray about the decision. But like untying a helium balloon and watching it bounce randomly off the walls, the excitement of the opportunity had quickly fizzled away, leaving him confused on his next move.

Chilled by the morning air, Brian woke up on the couch in the dark, still wearing his flannel shirt and jeans from yesterday. He didn't remember passing out the night before as he waited for his son to return. Sitting up, he rubbed a crick in his neck and hoped Daniel was asleep in his bed.

Just then, Daniel appeared from around the kitchen corner wearing his black sweat suit, running shoes and his green backpack. Headed by his Dad and out to the front door, he kept his eyes down, still looking to evade talking with his Dad.

"Daniel, wait buddy," Brian waved his hand, causing Daniel to stop walking. "I'm sorry about last night. I know Charlotte is important to you and I just got frustrated. Nobody seemed to be listening to me and at least giving this opportunity even a chance. Sooo…don't worry. We are not going to rush into anything." Brian's head dropped, realizing his bungled words probably did nothing to ease his son's mind.

"Ok," Daniel said without any emotion in his voice.

"What time is it?" Brian wondered since no sunlight peered thru the curtains.

"It's 5:30. I didn't sleep well so I'm going to start my run to school now and do some homework when I get there."

"Alright, well if you need a ride after practice, text me," Brian said while rubbing his eyes.

Daniel left without saying another word and Brian lay back down. Still tired, he wanted to go back to sleep but his mind began contemplating the job offer and unfortunately Maria's reaction. Now knowing sleep would escape him, he pried himself off the couch and started making breakfast for his family.

Right as Brian finished scrambling the eggs, Maria walked into the kitchen in her red cloth bathrobe and red slippers.

She yawned before asking softly, "Why didn't you come to bed last night?"

"I was waiting on Daniel to come back. And because I didn't want to fight any more about it," Brian said, turning away from her as he felt his frustration return.

Remembering the way the conversation ended, Maria said, "Hey, sorry for calling you stupid last night." She moved across the kitchen and hugged her husband from behind, hoping to end the strife.

Turning around, Brian put his arms around her and kissed her cheek, appreciating the apology. "Ok, but will you help me by praying about it? I am not sure what to do. I certainly don't want to just walk away from the opportunity of a lifetime without giving it serious consideration."

"Yes, you know I will. But I want you to apologize to Daniel," she said, moving over and sitting down at the dining room table.

"I already did this morning. He got up early for his run to school," Brian said, putting the eggs and toast on three plates.

"Geez, it must be freezing out there. Why does he like to do that?" Maria shuddered, thinking of jogging in the dark right now.

"I don't think he does. I think he is trying to discipline himself. It's good for him."

Suzy burst out of her bedroom in her pink pajamas and said huffily, "You guys are loud."

"Sorry Miss Grumpy, but you gotta get up anyway. Come eat your breakfast, ok?" Brian held a plate for her.

The juke box alarm went off in Suzy's bedroom, with Dad's newest selection, the Elvis' Hit Single, *Hound Dog*.

Brian immediately broke into a dance and sang along. "You aint nothing but a Hound Dog, Cryin all the time."

Suzy shook her head and said, "Dad, you bad at dancing."

This only encouraged Brian even more to dance as he slid across the laminate kitchen floor so he could sing into Suzy's face. "You ain't nothing but a Hound Dog, Cryin all the time."

Unimpressed, Suzy grabbed her forehead, saying, "Please change that song. It's annoying."

Maria chimed in, "You're right, hija. That song bugs me, too."

Brian pointed his finger at them and said in a deep voice trying to emulate Elvis, "Don't y'all ever talk about the King like that."

Quickly retreating to Suzy's bedroom, Maria turned off the music.

"Whew. Thanks Mom!" Suzy laughed and sat down at the table.

"Oh, you think I need your juke box. I can go all day long," he said before starting to sing the next line, "You can wag your tail but I aint gonna feed you no more."

In a formal protest, Suzy folded her arms on the dinner table in front of her plate and laid her head down on her arms.

"Ok, ok, I'll quit. Let's hurry and get ready, Snuzy."

Sitting at his big oak desk on Friday morning, Brian reminisced as he looked at the treasured wooden framed pictures on the wall next to him; one of Daniel holding a largemouth bass fish caught at a local lake; another capturing Suzy getting her face painted at the Harvest carnival; finally one of Maria and him in a canoe going down the Wasatchu river. In only ten years, they had become part of this small-town community and it felt like home.

However, the career advancement in front of him was essentially something he had worked for his whole life. Brian had wondered if God was opening a door for them, part of a better plan. So Maria and Brian had kept praying nightly over the past week and they both finally had peace about what to do next.

After Dialing the corporate cell phone of Red Farm Insurance Vice President Ed Hanson, Brian looked down, surprised to see his hand shaking.

"Hi, Mr. Hanson, it's Brian Beckham." He gripped the side of the desk to steady his hand.

"Great, Brian. I was expecting your call. Are we going to get you back in Atlanta?"

"Unfortunately, I will not be able to accept the position at this time. I want you to know that it has not been an easy decision, and I'm grateful to have been considered for the job.

"Wow. I'm surprised and disappointed. I cannot think of anyone more qualified than you and was looking to working more closely with you."

"Thank you for saying that. I'm sure you will find the right person."

"Do you mind if I ask why? I mean, that's quite an increase in pay you are turning down."

"Sure. The timing was just bad for my family. My kids are still in High School and it would be tough to uproot them. But we have come to love this little town, too. At the end, we decided that we don't want to just make a living. We are trying to make a life."

"Fair enough. You are a great asset to our company, and we appreciate all the hard work you put in. But I do need to hurry so I can let the board know to proceed with the other candidates."

"Thanks again Mr. Hanson, it's a privilege to work for you and Red Farm. I hope you have a great day."

The dark, gray sky did not change all morning, but the wind turned, blowing steadily from the south and making escape from the constant drizzle impossible.

After completing prenatal lab work a few days prior, the office of Dr. Karen Schwartz called Sherry to come back in for a follow up visit to review the results.

Dave could not get off work, so Sherry traveled alone for the school day appointment. Only a ten-minute drive, the office sat inside a converted three bedroom home near downtown. Dr. Schwartz was a very caring physician and highly regarded in the community of Gilmerton as an excellent OB-GYN. While not present for Sherry's first miscarriage, she held her during the second one, comforting Sherry as she wept.

Inside her office, the Doctor adjusted a black and white screen so Sherry could see it while lying down on the exam table. Initially shivering when the doctor applied the cold gel to her abdomen, Sherry warmed back up with the transducer probe moving across her belly. As they looked at the ultrasound together, the Doctor pointed to the baby, explaining to Sherry what they could see.

"Congratulations, your baby has officially graduated from embryo to fetus. This is the head as you probably know. If we could see clearer on this screen and had a better angle, we would see the baby's eye structures are completed, and even the tiny earlobes. Follow this line and you're seeing the arm. See the bend, that's the elbow. So already we are looking at your mini-me," Dr. Schwartz said, smiling at Sherry.

"Now let's crank up the volume and hear this heartbeat." Dr. Schwartz grabbed a dial on the machine and let it blast. "Wow, without even counting, we are listening to easily one hundred and fifty beats per minute."

Captivated by the image in front of her, it still seemed surreal to Sherry that this little body was inside her.

After letting her patient gaze at the screen for about fifteen seconds, the Doctor removed the probe and turned off the screen. "So Sherry, everything looks good. But I do have some concerns about some of these blood tests." Dr. Schwartz's thin eyebrows raised up as her face turned serious.

Sherry's stomach knotted up, making her nauseous. "About what?"

"Well, we call them markers. Most notably this high protein count." She locked eyes with Sherry, not shying away from the news she had to share.

"What would that mean?" Sherry asked, but not sure she wanted to know.

Crossing her arms, Dr. Schwartz paused. "It means your baby may have Down Syndrome."

Sherry sat silent and let her gaze fall to the floor so the Doctor continued, "We can do a non-invasive test in two weeks and that would come close to confirming it. We could know for certain by doing an Amniocentesis, but I don't recommend it due to your history of miscarriages. You will still have time to decide if you want to carry out the pregnancy. Now the NIPT will be a simple blood sample we can get from your arm and we will be looking for the chromosomal abnormalities, like trisomy 21....."

As soon as the Doctor went into the technical aspect of the test, Sherry tried to pay attention, but her mind sprinted too far ahead, barely understanding anything Dr. Schwartz said. She tuned back in as the doctor had almost finished talking.

"So let's schedule you for two weeks from now and we will know more. But everything looks good right now, Sherry. Try not to worry," she said and turned to leave.

Try not to worry? Clearly you don't know me. I will be worrying the next fourteen days. Good Lord, why can't things ever go smoothly? She thought.

After walking out to the receptionist desk, Sherry made the appointment before ambling out to her car. She needed to talk to someone. She wanted desperately to talk to Dave, but he was still teaching at school.

Once inside her car, she decided to call her best friend and roommate in college Tori Myers. Also a former Florida Gator cheerleader, Tori's gregarious and competitive personality helped her become super successful, now working as Marketing Director for Marriott Hotels in Orlando, Florida.

Dialing her at mid-day, Sherry wasn't sure if she could reach Tori on her cell phone, but she picked up on the second ring.

"Sherry! Long time roomie!" Tori exclaimed in her high pitch, mousey voice.

"Did I reach you at a good time? Sorry to call you during the business day."

"Not a problem. I am just eating a salad and looking at some print ads we are about to run." Tori always talked a mile a minute and Sherry didn't know if she would be able to even discuss with her about why she called. Tori continued, "We just opened a new Marriott in St. Augustine. You guys gotta come down. I can get you a free suite. We would love to see you."

"You and Scott?" Sherry wondered if she remembered correctly.

"No, girl. That ship has sailed. I've been with Carlos for the last nine months. Things are going great. He's a car import dealer from Madrid."

"Oh, that's good," Sherry said, rubbing her forehead and questioning if Tori was the person she should be talking to right now.

"What's new with you? I can't believe it's been ages since we talked."

"Well, I was just at my OB- GYN and looking at an ultrasound of our baby."

"Congratulations, Sherry! That's great. Are y'all excited?"

"Yes, but…" Sherry hesitated, not sure if she wanted to divulge the Doctor's concerns. "I called you because I need someone to talk to. I haven't told anyone else this yet, not even Dave. So please keep this confidential."

Tori slowed her words. "You know you can trust me, Sherry."

"They think the baby may have Down Syndrome. We won't know for sure for a couple of weeks," Sherry said, letting out a big breath.

"Are you going to tell Dave?"

Tori's question caught Sherry by surprise. Instead of answering, she decided to ask Tori, "Um, why wouldn't I tell Dave?"

"Well, that way you can still choose if you want to keep it. If he doesn't know, it will be solely your choice like it should be. Hold on for a second. Thanks, Jackson, tell them I will email them the specs and call them in five minutes. Sherry, I'm so sorry hon, but I gotta go. But let's talk more about this. I will be gone this weekend, but we can talk anytime." Just like that, everything was back to business for Tori, the only world she really knew.

"Okay, thanks," she finished and hung up. Staring at the tiny raindrops piling up on her windshield, Sherry really wasn't thankful to have talked to Tori, just more scared and confused. And somewhat ashamed. For Sherry didn't admit to Tori a couple of things. The more she thought about it, the less she wanted to talk to Dave about the Doctor's concerns. And while she never kept any secrets from him before, she wasn't about to confess to anyone her consideration to possibly abort the baby.

Friday night at the Beckham's round dinner table sat an array of lettuce, tomatoes, buns and freshly grilled beef patties. As usual, Suzy gave her hamburger a bath in ketchup, neglecting the vegetable toppings her parents presented. Maria brought a bowl of spinach and kale salad to the table and sat next to Brian. He grabbed Maria's hand and was about to say grace as Daniel walked in the front door.

"Oh good, Daniel, just in time for dinner," Brian said, inviting him over to the table.

"Uh, I'm not hungry," he mumbled, avoiding eye contact and wanting to walk past to his bedroom.

"I need you to stay at the table, Daniel. I have some news you'll want to hear," Brian added.

Daniel pulled his backpack off and put it on the floor before sitting in the chair between Suzy and his dad.

"First, I want to pray." Brian continued, and they all bowed their heads. "Lord, I want to thank you for this family, always providing for us and always being good to us. In Jesus Name."

Suzy yelled her customary, "Amen, let's eat!" and began engulfing her hamburger.

"Don't eat too fast, Suzy. And I want you to eat a salad, too, ok?" Maria said, touching her arm.

"So what's with the news, Dad?" Daniel said, and began chewing on his index fingernail.

"Well, your Mom and I have been praying all week and after weighing everything out, we decided not to accept the job offer and move to Atlanta."

Daniel leapt out of his chair and embraced his dad. Always quick to get caught up in the emotion, Suzy jumped up as well and began hugging Daniel from behind with a Kung Fu grip on her hamburger.

"Suzy! You are getting ketchup on Daniel's back. Siente te, hija." Maria said, telling her to sit down.

"I take it you're stoked on the decision," Brian said smiling as his son released his hug.

"Yes. Yes I am. Now I gotta jump in the shower. I'm meeting Charlotte and some friends. But I'll grab a burger to go," Daniel said quickly, picking up his backpack and headed to his bedroom.

"So we stay here, Dad?" Suzy said with ketchup smeared on her face.

"Yes, we are gonna keep living here, honey."

"So I can be a cheerleader!" Suzy thrust her arms in the air.

Brian reached across the table to hand her a paper napkin. "Well, we need those lil' feet of yours healed up first," Brian said.

"I'm trying, Dad." Suzy said before wiping her face.

"I know you are, girl. Did your new orthotics help at school today?"

"No, they hurt my feet more." Suzy's face turned sour when reminded of the uncomfortable insoles.

"What?" Brian said, glancing to Maria with concern in his eyes.

"Give them a few days, hija. Your feet need to get used to them." Maria offered.

"But I hate them. My feet hurt really bad today."

Brian tried to lighten the mood. "Ok, well after dinner, your mom said she would give you and me a foot massage."

Maria shook her head to the side in disagreement. "Pfftttt.... You're dreaming, Mister Beckham. I'll give my sweet Suzy one."

Suzy smiled at Maria. "You always tickle my feet, Mama."

"'Cause I love to hear you laugh, hija." Maria leaned over and kissed her on the cheek.

All weekend, the stress caused Sherry to resort back to her old habit of trying to stay busy for the sake of staying busy. By immersing herself in all kinds of tasks, she hoped to avoid thinking about the possible health problems her baby faced.

After grocery shopping in the morning, she cleaned the deck and the garage on Sunday afternoon. Dave noticed the constant activity, asking her if everything was okay, and concerned since he had seen this movie before. Not wanting to alarm Dave, she played it straight by claiming she was simply trying to get ahead and not procrastinate on her 'to do' list.

But all the bustling about took its toll and by Monday morning she was exhausted. Looking at her reflection in the bathroom mirror above the sink, she noticed the bags under her eyes and decided to have a pep talk to herself before the workday.

"Enough of this. You need to chill out. You're worried about things that may not even happen. Sherry Tinsdale, you are gonna stay cool, calm and collected. We need you to stay present."

Walking down the hallway, Dave heard talking coming from the bathroom. The door was halfway open, and he saw Sherry standing in front of the mirror. He stuck his head in the door and looked at her through the mirror, asking, "Who are you talking to?"

"Just the Best American History teacher in all of Kings County," Sherry claimed.

"Do you have Jed Fullerton from Roland High School on speaker phone?" Dave quipped.

Sherry flashed a smirk at Dave in the mirror. "Oh Dave, your jealousy is quite flattering."

Later at West End High School, Sherry was surprised that the self-pep talk actually helped improve her mood for the day. After fourth period, she headed to the teachers' lounge for coffee. Approaching the Home Ec class, she saw Billy Martin standing near the door.

"Hi Billy, where're the kids?" Sherry asked, noticing the empty room thru the glass window of the door.

"They are walking around the football field and should be back in twenty minutes. How is everything going with Suzy?"

"Well, she was learning some basics, but started having feet problem so now her parents told her she can only watch."

"Aww, man. She has been complaining when we go on our trips downtown. Right now she is sitting in the stands while the other kids do some laps. I guess they just got her new orthopedic insoles last week, so hopefully that will help."

"Yeah, the girls were so excited to get her on the field with them, but the season is coming to an end soon, so I don't know...but hey, I was curious, how did you decide to teach Special Ed?"

"I have a cousin that is the same age as me who has Down Syndrome. I used to go to birthday parties with kids who had all kinds of disabilities and was able to interact with them. I saw the difference the teachers made in my cousin's development and just felt like this would be really rewarding."

"Well…" Sherry hesitated before asking, "Has it lived up to your expectations?"

"Beyond my expectations. These kids teach me things no one else could. Every day. I get more from them than they ever get from me."

"Now you're just being modest." Sherry smiled.

"No, I'm dead serious. These kids are so non-judgmental. Like, they always see other people through a child's eyes. They really care about each other. And man, they have to overcome major obstacles. Who doesn't pull for the underdog, right?"

Sherry nodded in agreement.

"But I ain't gonna lie. It can be very tiring and taxing at times. And I can't imagine how hard it is for some of these parents. I've known several through the years who had to change their jobs so they could take care of their kid. They have to be one hundred percent committed, one hundred percent of the time."

"Wow." Sherry said flatly, letting her eyes drift toward the outside window as she considered what Billy just said.

"So, why did you become a History teacher?" Billy asked.

Through the windows, they both saw the kids from his class walking up to the door that leads outside so Sherry knew she needed to leave.

"Well, I will tell you that story in our next chat," she said quickly and exited into the hallway.

Gaining some good insight into having a disabled child from Billy, Sherry decided that instead of finding tasks to just occupy her time, she would do the homework, researching for more information online about what others had to say on the subject.

Chapter 7

Tuesday morning, Brian and Maria Beckham were not awakened by the alarm juke box in Suzy's room, but by the sounds of muffled crying coming from their daughter's room. The night before, Suzy had cried herself to sleep and now her parents were startled that the pain had seemingly returned. Quickly getting out of their bed, Brian and Maria rushed to Suzy's room, finding her sitting up on the bed with her feet dangling off the side.

Maria sat on the bed next to Suzy, putting her arm around her while Brian kneeled down, looking at her tiny disfigured feet. Even after they tried to ice them for her last night, they were still as blue and swollen this morning.

"Suzy, your feet still hurt?" Brian asked, assuming this is why she cried.

"Yes. They woke me up." She whimpered, her face flush and nose running.

Brian took off his white t-shirt and used it to wipe his daughter's nose. "I'm gonna get you some aspirin, ok."

"No!" Suzy yelled, slamming her hands on the mattress. She absolutely hated taking pills.

Brian said gently, but trying to be firm. "Suzy, do you want your feet to feel better? You need to take some medicine. We can mix it in some applesauce for you…"

Maria interrupted, "I'm going to call the bus and tell them not to come get her." She got up to go grab her cell phone from the bedroom.

Curious and wanting to test her feet, Brian asked her, "Can you let Daddy hold your foot?"

"No! It hurts bad," Suzy said through her constant sniffing.

"What's wrong with Suzy?" Daniel asked, appearing in her doorway.

"Her feet are still hurting. I've never seen them this bad." Brian answered as the juke alarm clock came on and he quickly reached over to hit the snooze button.

"Oh, Chiquita. I hope you feel better. Te quiero," he said he loved her in Spanish before turning to leave for school.

Suzy didn't respond, keeping her stare downward, too focused on the pain.

Maria returned to the room after notifying the bus. "What are we going to do? Her big dance is next Friday night," Maria asked, looking at Brian.

He let out a big sigh. "I don't know. When the office is open, we should call the Orthopedic."

"Ok, but let's pray for her now," Maria stated.

Nodding in agreement, he placed his hand on Suzy's head while Maria put her hand on Suzy's shoulder. Their daughter was used to seeing her parents pray for her since she was a toddler.

Brian prayed out loud, "Dear Lord, we pray for wisdom to know what we should do. We know you give us doctors to be your healing hands. Help us know whether to get the surgery now. Please help and guide us."

Maria followed up with her prayer. "Heavenly Father, we thank you so much for our precious daughter. You know how much joy she brings us. Right now, we come to you and ask for a miracle healing. Please touch her feet so she can walk without pain. We ask this in the mighty name of Jesus. Amen."

"Amen. Now, Suzy, you lay down and take the weight off your feet. I'm going to go make you breakfast," Brian said softly, before he and Maria went to the kitchen to talk more.

Taking some eggs out of the refrigerator, Brian began cracking them into a bowl while Maria stood beside him leaning against the black tile countertop. Keeping his voice low, Brian asked, "Why do you think the bunions are flaring so badly? Those insoles don't seem to be helping at all."

"I don't know. I even put a toe spacer on her yesterday morning for added relief, so I was surprised she was in so much pain," Maria, her wide eyes revealing exasperation.

Brian shook his head and began beating the eggs. He took out a frying pan, flipped the dial on the stove top, and while waiting for it to heat up, turned back to Maria. "Should we call the foundation and let them know she can't come to the dance next Friday?"

Maria pursed her lips before saying, "That's gonna be so disappointing. We've been helping plan this since April."

Suddenly out of the corner of his eye, Brian saw Suzy standing in the hallway at the edge of the dining room.

"I can still dance," she stated plainly.

Looking down at her barefoot on the ceramic tile floor, Brian exhorted her. "Suzy, you need to be in bed and off your feet."

"Feet better." Moving toward them, she did a little skip to demonstrate, and finished with a high kick for emphasis. "See?"

Her parents both stood stunned for a few seconds before Maria asked, "Did the aspirin help?"

"I didn't give her any," Brian said, rubbing his head in disbelief. "Suzy, let us see you walk."

"Like this?" she smiled, pretending to be walking in slow motion toward her room before turning around and coming back to the kitchen.

The front door burst open as Daniel rushed in, sweating profusely and panting. Seeing his dad, he said quickly, "Dang, I got half a mile and realized I left a book. Can you give me a ride?"

When he got to the kitchen, he was surprised to see Suzy standing there and his parents looking like they were in shock. "I thought Suzy's feet were hurting?" Daniel blurted out.

"They were," Maria's voice quivered, her eyes beginning to water. "Daniel, I think God just healed her feet."

"See. Feet better," Suzy said, pointing a foot at Daniel.

Turning off the stove, Brian walked over to where Suzy now stood, stooping before her to scrutinize her feet closer. "Put your foot on my thigh, Snuz, so Daddy can see it."

Daniel and Maria peered over Brian's shoulder so they could inspect the feet closer for themselves.

After holding the foot in his hand, the same one Suzy would not let him touch earlier, Brian concluded, "So look, there's no redness or even any swelling. It's as if the bunions are not even pointy like before but the bones look all rounded off. I can't even believe my eyes."

"I think you don't wanna believe, Brian," Maria added.

Brian glanced back over his shoulder. "C'mon, cut me some slack. It's not like I don't wanna believe. This is crazy. I know God can heal, but I just uh... I mean, is this just temporary? I don't know what to think."

"Brian, I told you we have to believe He will answer our prayers. I know our first instincts are to get medicine and call the Doctors, but we have to let God do His thing."

"You're right, honey. Honestly, I just still can't believe what I'm seeing. And I'm trying to be cautiously optimistic and pragmatic here. No one will be happier than me if God healed her completely. Bottom line is right now Suzy's standing in front of us without pain."

"Daniel, wanna kiss my foot?" Suzy joked.

"Chiquita, you don't need to worry about that happening. Ever." Daniel replied with a straight face, always enjoying the banter with his sister.

Slowly putting her foot down, Brian stood up. "Okay girl go get dressed. I will make y'all breakfast and take you to school."

Daniel put his hand on Brian's shoulder, saying, "Well Dad, it looks like Mom has more faith than you," causing his Dad to chuckle.

Maria smiled and messed with Daniel's hair. "Let's pray. Thank you, Lord for healing our girl. Help us with our unbelief so that we remember that nothing is impossible with you!" she proclaimed.

Home Economics Special Ed at West End School was strategically placed at 11 A.M. every day before lunch period so the kids could enjoy the fruit of their labor after class. Billy Martin looked forward to watching the kids create their own meals, even the culinary disasters. This day was no different as he paced around in the kitchen area of the classroom.

"Ok, besides me, who else in the Magnificent Seven is ready to make a pizza?"

All the kids raised their hands, but Josh pumped his fist in the air, yelling, "Oh, yeah! I'm ready!"

This week's hair color choice for Josh was an electric orange and his throwback punk band t-shirt of the day revealed 'Minor Threat'.

"Yoohoo! I am glad someone is enthusiastic about it," Billy said. "Everybody come to the prep table and stand in front of your personal size pizza. You'll see they already have the sauce on the dough for you."

When the kids had gathered around a large 12x4, black top table, Billy continued with his instructions. "You see in front of your pizza all the different bowls filled with mushrooms, pepperoni, onions, peppers and cheese. Now all you have to do is build your own special pie. Take some ingredients out of a bowl. Some! Not the whole bowl, Josh." When Billy emphasized Josh's name, all the kids laughed, including Josh. "Then pass the bowl to the person next to you. After you put all your toppings on, I will announce which pizza wins the awards for most creative and most delicious looking before I put them in the preheated oven. Ok?"

When Katie passed the onion bowl to Earl on her right, he noticed among the chopped onions a long slice that had missed being cut. Not liking the disorder the lone strand was causing in the bowl, Earl plucked the slice out of the bowl and tossed it into the air. The slice made it to the head of the table, landing on top of Billy's ear. Knowing a few of the kids had noticed the errant flight of the onion slice, Billy pretended as if it wasn't there. The kids begin to elbow each other, pointing at the onion dangling from their teacher's ear, snickering at his seeming unawareness.

Finally Katie felt bad for her teacher and said, "Uh, Mister Billy, you have onion on your ear."

All the kids now looked at Billy and began laughing out loud.

"What? How did this get here? I took a shower this morning?" Billy removed the onion and looked carefully to inspect it as if it would give him more clues as to its origins.

Using her hands to demonstrate, Katie then explained to her teacher, "Earl didn't like so he tossed it."

Imitating the voice of an airline pilot making an announcement to the passengers, Billy declared, "Attention Mister Earl and fellow students, please make sure to put all unwanted food into the trash can next time. Thank you in advance for your cooperation."

"Ok, ok," Earl replied, nodding his head and returning his focus to the task in front of him.

After allowing them five minutes to apply different toppings, Billy said it was time for him to judge the pizzas.

Billy approached Justin who moved his wheelchair back so his teacher could get a better look at his work. While from the side it looked like Justin was wearing a beaver trooper style hat with fur sidebars, a closer look revealed Justin was wearing a Star Wars Chewbacca hat.

"Justin, your pizza looks like the force is with you. Everything is evenly distributed, and you have made me instantly hungry. Good job."

Billy moved on to the next pie. "Now Earl, you too did a good job of covering your pizza evenly with all the toppings. But what is up with all these pieces of pepperoni piled up on each other in the center?"

"Mister Billy, it's a pizza in the middle of my pizza," Earl declared, flapping his hands rapidly in front of him.

"Why didn't I think of that? I will be stealing that idea. Good job, Mister Earl," Billy said before sliding over to Katie's pie.

"Ok, Miss Katie. I see you stuck to your vegetarian diet and strategically placed everything in a delicious fashion. Job well done." Billy's comment made Katie smile as she adjusted her glasses.

The teacher moved around to the other side of the table, facing the student who wore the T-Shirt with one giant word that read, 'Faith'. "Well, what do we have here Mister Buster? You have designed a perfect smiley face with all this pepperoni. I like it. High five my main man." Billy and Buster slapped each other's hands.

"And it looks like someone else over here got all creative with the pepperoni. What in the world could this giant S possibly stand for?" Billy asked, but knowing the answer.

"It stands for Suzy, Mister Billy!" Suzy exclaimed, clearly proud of her work.

"Oh, I thought it stood for Super Woman," Billy said, scratching his head and feigning confusion.

With her hands on her hips now, she clarified, "No. It stands for Suzy. I just told you."

"You did just tell me. I stand corrected," Billy quipped.

"Next time you listen," Suzy cracked a smile, always saying that line to her teacher whenever she could.

Billy chuckled. "Next time I will listen. But I think we all know that S stands for sassy," Billy stated as he moved to the final pizza.

"Ok, what is this giant mountain of goodness we looking at here now?" Billy inquired of Josh's pizza.

"Everything!" Josh yelled, eager to dig into his colossal creation.

"It does appear to have everything and more. You took 'The Works' to a whole notha level," Billy raised his hand above his head, showing where the bar had been set. "This thing looks straight outta the Anarchist Cookbook."

"Yep," Josh smiled proudly, yet Billy was confident he did not get the reference to the real book that punk rockers used to love to read.

"Ok, the judges have decided and the results are in. Please hold your applause until all two of the awards are announced. Most delicious looking pizza goes to Mister Justin and with most creative pizza going to Mister Buster. Congratulations to all the contestants and you all get an A," Billy declared, and the kids all began clapping.

"I'm starving!" Suzy said, before jumping a couple feet away from the table and doing a high kick.

"Whoa! Are your feet feeling better, Suzy?" Billy said, surprised to see her put all her weight on one foot.

"Feet better, Mister Billy. My mama and dad prayed for me."

"Well, that's awesome. I'm glad to hear it. Now let's get these in the oven and celebrate with some pizza pie."

While Sherry had experienced some morning sickness only a couple hours earlier in the day, she felt like she could finally eat something now that she was in downtown Gilmerton. Entering the bagel shop, the same college age kid with the nose ring who messed up her previous visit stood before the counter. His nervous glance told her he remembered their encounter.

"Hi, I would like the spinach and cheese bagel, toasted, and an orange juice, please," Sherry said, looking into her purse, avoiding eye contact with the clerk.

"Sure. I know for sure we have some fresh ones so it will only be a few minutes," he politely said.

After receiving her order, Sherry decided to drop a twenty-dollar bill into the pint sized glass tip jar. The clerk was reaching for some napkins below the countertop and when he stood up, he immediately noticed the only tip in the jar.

"Hey, thanks a lot," he said, smiling at Sherry.

"You're very welcome. Thanks for the good service," Sherry added, and smiled back.

Sherry felt good that she had been able to make amends for insulting the kid on her last visit. The sun was beginning to warm the morning air, so she decided to enjoy her food on the wooden patio outside the store, sitting down under an umbrella covered table. Located on Main Street a few blocks from the square downtown, the patio was on the side of the shop, facing the street and with access to the adjacent parking lot. Two pigeons jumped from table to table, looking for scraps and while they eyed Sherry's bagel, they kept a safe distance.

Not five minutes later, Maria Beckham's car pulled in the spot next to Sherry's vehicle.

Suzy climbed out of the passenger's seat and immediately became very animated. "Coach Sherry! What are you doing here? Mom, it's Coach Sherry," Suzy pointed toward the patio as her Mom shut the car door.

"Hey guys, what are y'all up to?" Sherry asked as they approached her.

Walking on to the patio, Maria said, "Hi Sherry, we are just gonna meet some friends on their farm so Suzy can watch the horses. I'm just grabbing some bagels before we head out there."

"Sounds fun. Are you excited?" She asked, looking at Suzy.

"Yes, I love to watch horses. But I'm scared to ride."

"Well, they are really tall," Sherry said. "I fell off a horse when I was about your age. Luckily it was on the beach so the sand made for a softer landing."

"Whoa," Suzy said in amazement.

Maria handed her daughter a twenty-dollar bill and sent her inside to get their order that Maria had placed on-line.

"I feel Suzy can actually start practicing cheer again. It was miraculous….," Maria stopped, not knowing if Sherry would believe the story.

"Oh wow. Well, we can see how it goes. Our last football game is in two weeks, but maybe we can still get her on the field."

"Her little heart would explode with joy if that happens. She has been walking around pain free for the last three days, so we are hoping she'll be okay now."

Feeling bold and knowing there would be no one better to give her the insight she desired, Sherry asked, "Can I ask you something personal?"

Maria sat down across from Sherry. Despite their lighthearted conversation, she sensed something was troubling the coach and Maria wanted to help.

"I'll try to be as transparent as I can, Sherry. What's your question?"

Sherry stared down at the table for a few seconds, pausing before she spoke. She wanted to choose her words carefully, not revealing she was actually inquiring for herself before looking up.

"I have a friend who is pregnant with a Down Syndrome baby. She is pretty scared about all the unknowns."

Before Maria could answer, Suzy came back out thru the exit door onto the patio with a big box of bagels and cream cheese.

"Sweetie, take them to the car and listen to some music on your headphones while I talk to Coach Sherry, ok?"

"Ok, Mama. Can I eat in the car?"

"Yes, but be careful not to make a mess, hija," Maria said before turning back to the coach.

"Well Sherry, it was pretty scary for me. My husband and I never even knew anyone who had Downs before we had Suzy. And our doctor didn't really help alleviate any of our fears either. He told us that something like fifty percent of Downs babies are born with heart and lung problems. At times, I honestly felt like he was pushing us to abort the baby."

Putting her fingertips over her lips, Sherry nodded back in empathy.

"We just really didn't know what to expect. I even went through a period where I felt like God was cursing me for all the bad things I had done. When I tried to pray, it felt like God was silent. It was as if He was testing my faith. Then when she was born, it was as if He was testing my patience. We were super happy that she didn't have any major health issues, but I am not gonna sugar coat it. There were some tough times. It took forever before she could even crawl. She didn't get potty-trained until she was five years old. I think it was like three and half years before she could even say basic words. Not being able to communicate with your child is so difficult because you need to know what is wrong."

Losing her appetite, Sherry slid her bagel away from her. Everything ~~Maria~~ just said only compounded own her own fears.

"The Down Syndrome kids' immune systems are weaker and Suzy almost died when she was two from pneumonia."

"Oh my gosh," Sherry said, before being distracted by the noise of people yelling. Both she and Maria turned their eyes to the sidewalk on Main Street where a homeless woman and a dog walked toward them.

A pickup truck had slowed down and there was a heated exchange between her and the driver. Suddenly the truck tires squealed as it sped off while the lady saluted the truck with a one finger wave. The woman continued rambling, mumbling loudly, before turning left into the parking lot of the bagel shop and walking in front of the patio where they sat.

Suzy rapidly got out of her car seat and ran up to the lady, waving at her with a half-eaten bagel in hand.

"Lucy! I got you some food!" she said, kneeling before the dog and petting her like an old friend. Turning her head up to the patio, Suzy yelled, "Look Mama, its Lucy the dog."

"Hi Suzy, you remember me?" the lady asked.

Suzy stood up. "Yes, your name is Alice. Do you want a bagel?"

Hearing their conversation, Maria nodded at Suzy, pointing her finger toward the car so she would know to go retrieve a bagel.

"Um, that's nice of you sweetheart, but you don't have to…." Alice stopped as Suzy interrupted her.

"Hold on and I get you one," she said quickly as she walked back to the car.

Alice looked back and smiled awkwardly at Sherry and Maria.

After Suzy handed a blueberry bagel to Alice, she kneeled back down and began petting the dog again. "Mama, Lucy is a good dog," Suzy yelled.

"I can see. You have a beautiful dog, Alice," Maria said.

Without looking back, she said quickly, "Thank you, kindly. But I have to go now. Y'all have a good day. Come on, Lucy." Alice tugged on the leash.

"Ok, see ya later, Alice. See ya later, Lucy." Suzy said, standing back up, waving at them while they walked away. Heading back inside the car, Suzy put her headphones on and immediately began bobbing her head back and forth to the music.

Sherry turned to Maria; her eyes wide open in amazement. "How does Suzy know that lady?"

"I don't know. She seems to know everybody in this town. And she always remembers their names. It's unbelievable," Maria said smiling with pride.

"You know all the hard things we have gone through with her; you can basically have the same problems with kids without disabilities. You just have to be more patient with the Downs kids because they take longer to learn things. And the school programs they have now to help these kids are amazing. Suzy has come a long way. We are really pleased with her. I mean, like with that homeless lady, you see how compassionate and kindhearted she is. But come to think of it, have you ever met a mean-spirited Downs kid?" Maria asked, tilting her head to the side, trying to recollect if her statement was as true as she remembered.

Maria continued, "These kids are special not because that is some euphemism for handicapped. They really do have big hearts. When Suzy becomes your friend, she considers you a friend for life. I mean, that's how she looks at you Sherry. At home, she tells us all the time that Coach Sherry is my homie," Maria said and started laughing.

"She does? That's hilarious." Sherry smiled.

"We are constantly cracking up at all the funny things she says and does. She is always the life of the party. But I've been reflecting lately about how many things she has taught us. When life gets all hectic and stressful, Suzy helps remind me to be content. While at one time I thought that her birth was some kind of curse, it has turned out to be a huge blessing for us. I wouldn't want Suzy to be anyone else than who she is."

"Wow, that's neat. I'll pass this info on to my friend." Sherry rubbed her chin in a contemplative pose.

"Tell her to call me. I would love to talk to her and encourage her," Maria said, standing up and headed to the car.

"I will. Thanks so much for the talk. And I'm still holding you to those empanadas.

"Pronto amiga. Yo prometo," Maria said, promising soon.

Friday afternoon, the final school bell had rung ten minutes ago and Sherry sat alone at her desk. She would need to leave in a couple of hours to make it in time for the final away game in Colbert County. Deciding not to car-pool with any of the girls on the team, Sherry wanted privacy in case she was driving and got the phone call from her OB-GYN, confirming the final test results. The last two weeks seemed like the longest waiting period of her life, but at last she hoped to know for certain if her baby had Downs.

Knowing the call might come in any minute, she constantly looked at her watch while slowly twirling the wedding band around her finger, trying to ignore that the real source of her agony was a restless conscience.

She felt terrible about keeping all this a secret from Dave and wished she had told him from the beginning. Part of her wanted to call him before he left for a scheduled oil change, and just spill her guts. She wouldn't blame him one bit if he were angry with her. But the other part rationalized that ultimately this was her choice, consequences be damned.

She pulled out her phone and went on her Facebook account to help distract her whirling thoughts when a tap at her classroom door startled her. The door cracked open and Math teacher Gilda Cohen stuck her head in.

"Sherry, the secret's out!" Gilda declared.

"What?" Sherry nervously shifted in her chair, wondering if anyone knew about her pregnancy.

"We have a huge celebrity on campus. Come with me." Gilda said turning away, waving her hand for Sherry to follow.

Relieved that Gilda was referring to something else, Sherry welcomed the diversion, curious as to what famous person would bother to visit Gilmerton and followed Gilda out to the hallway.

Catching up to her fellow teacher, Sherry asked, "Any idea who it is?"

"Yes, and rumor has it, he is a Florida Gator Legend."

"I went to the University of Florida," Sherry said proudly.

"I know. That's why I came and got you. But I won't tell you because I want to see if the suspense will kill you before we get there," Gilda quipped.

The joke made Sherry shake her head. "Gilda, you are the worst."

"Guilty," Gilda said, grinning as they walked quickly down the hallway.

Once they reached the bus drop off area by the gym entrance, their eyes were drawn to the white stretch limousine that sat idling by the curb with a small crowd around the back of the vehicle. As Gilda and Sherry slowed their approach to the limo, they saw the back of a broad-shouldered man wearing a black tuxedo, towering above the students gathered around him. Once the pictures and autographs were received, the kids walked away satisfied and Sherry peered closer.

Her mouth went wide when she recognized the man's face. "Oh my goodness, Tim Tebow!"

"Sherry Caspar?" Tebow asked, but confident he knew her.

"Yes, well, it's Sherry Tinsdale now. How are you old, buddy?" she reached over and gave Tim a hug.

"Wait, you actually know him?" said Gilda, more surprised that Sherry knew him personally than that the famous Heisman Trophy Winner was standing in front of her.

"Sherry was Senior Captain of the cheerleader squad when I was a junior," Tim remembered.

"And Tim led us to the National Championship Title. MVP of the title game." Sherry's face lit up.

"We had a great team," Tim smiled, trying to deflect the accomplishments off of him. Famous for his humility, Tim endeared even opposing fans.

"My husband and I love watching your commentary on college football. So, what brings you to the bustling metropolis of Gilmerton?" Gilda asked.

"To pick up my big date. And here she comes now." Tim pointed toward the gym and began walking toward his date.

Gilda and Sherry turned around and saw Suzy in a red prom dress being accompanied by her parents.

Tim rushed over and introduced himself. "Hi Suzy, I'm Tim and I will be escorting you to The Ball. I got you a corsage in the Limo. We will have your parents follow us over to Big Lake Resort, ok?"

Suzy nodded and Maria spoke to Tim, "Thank you so much for coming all the way out here. This is amazing."

"My pleasure, guys. Suzy, where are the rest of the kids?" Tim asked.

"Coming." As quick as she said that, the missing members of the Magnificent Seven rounded the Gym corner, all dressed to the nines. While local hairdressers helped to style their hair, the Tim Tebow Foundation had provided the suits and gowns for the kids. The dance event known as the *Night to Shine* had become an international celebration.

Tebow extended his arm, bent it at the elbow, and allowed Suzy to hook her hand in the nook as he escorted her to the Limo.

Approaching the car, Suzy yelled, "Hi Coach Sherry. We're gonna dance!" She stopped walking and unleashed a high kick.

"Whoa, Suzy!" Tim's eyes went big. "Did Coach Sherry teach you that?"

"No, Suzy taught herself that. She's a natural," Sherry said.

"Well, jump in the Limo and I will join you in a minute, Suzy." Tim said and waited to greet the rest of her classmates as they got closer.

Sherry and Gilda were watching Tebow high five each kid as they piled into the limo, when Sherry's cellphone rang. Looking down at the phone screen, Sherry recognized the number and her heart stopped.

"Gilda, I have to take this." Sherry walked away quickly, trying to put some distance between herself and anyone who might be in earshot of the call.

Walking back toward her classroom, Sherry took a deep breath and then answered the phone, "Dr. Cohen?"

"Yes, Sherry. Did I reach you at a good time?

"Yes, I can talk. Were you able to get the test results back yet?" Sherry began to nibble on her fingertip as she approached a vacant hallway.

"I just received them an hour ago. Would you like to meet with me on Monday? I can set some time aside."

Her answer made Sherry's stomach churn and caused her to stop walking. "Dr. Cohen, I don't want to wait till Monday. I just want to know what you know."

"Okay. I understand. The DNA tests shows your baby most likely has Down Syndrome."

Sherry put her hand on her forehead and took a step back. After a brief pause, the Doctor continued.

"I'd like to get you back in for a visit next week so we can give you additional information and go over your options..." she said, before Sherry cut her off.

"Doctor, I need to get off the phone. I'll call you next week. Thanks for calling me back," she said hurriedly.

"Okay, Sherry, good night." Click.

Dizzy, Sherry placed her hand up against the wall to stabilize herself, standing still for a few minutes. Finally feeling like she could move, she started walking in a daze back to her class to retrieve her keys and purse. Once out at her vehicle, she went into auto-pilot mode, and drove toward Colbert County.

On the two-lane county road heading out of town along the Wasatchu River, a news program blared over the car speakers, but her mind went blank and Sherry only heard a few sentences. After about twenty minutes of driving, the initial shock of the Doctor's call began to wear off and she became emotionally overwhelmed. Sherry looked in the rearview mirror and saw that her now pale white face was covered in sweat. Feeling claustrophobic and nauseous, she quickly pulled over to a boat launch to get out into the fresh air.

Gravel flew off the bottom of her car as she came to a sudden stop. A couple of men loading their kayak into the back of a pickup truck stared at her curiously. Getting out of her car, she ignored them and walked over to the water's edge. She looked downstream through the lush canyon at the rapids boiling over the rocks, hoping the stillness of the river would calm her frazzled nerves.

Instead, the negative input she had heard recently about having a disabled child flooded her mind. She started remembering things like Billy saying how he could not imagine how 'difficult it is for some of his student's parents, some even forced to change their jobs'. She recalled the statistic of 'fifty percent of Downs's infants having lung and heart problems.'

For the past two weeks, Sherry had gathered all kinds of information. From research on medical webpages to talking with Maria and Billy. She memorized her list of pros and cons. Even with all that knowledge, all the different variables kept her confused on what their life would look like. Suddenly a cool breeze swept through the canyon, causing her to shudder from the chilled air. As she hugged her stomach to warm herself, she was confronted with the reality of the living baby between her arms, and a flood of guilt rushed over her.

What about how this would impact my baby? Sherry thought.

Sherry had been so self-absorbed about how this would affect her that ultimately she neglected to think about the impact on her baby. The very baby she desperately wanted for so long.

Now shivering from the setting of the sun, Sherry hurried back to the warmth of her car. As soon as she closed the door, the story of Tim Tebow's mom came to her mind. The story had not even crossed her mind since she heard it ten years ago at a church service in Gainesville, Florida.

In front of a large congregation, Pam Tebow had recounted her pregnancy complications that led Doctors to believe it would be a still birth. Because Pam's health was in danger, the Doctors recommended abortion. But Pam decided she would trust the Lord and see her baby born. Without her act of faith, Sherry realized that there would be no Tim Tebow. And over an hour ago, Tim Tebow would not have been in Gilmerton, Georgia taking a Down Syndrome girl to a dance.

At this point, to say this was all merely chance or coincidence was something Sherry could no longer accept. God finally had Sherry Tinsdale's full attention.

With her eyes welling over with tears, Sherry could not contain herself. "God, forgive me! I'm sorry for being so selfish. Forgive me for forgetting how good you are." Putting one hand on her stomach, she prayed, "Thank you for this child. Please protect this baby and give me a chance to be a good mother. In Your Name."

By humbly crying out to God, all of the anxiety instantly left her, and Sherry finally felt a sense of clarity that she had lacked for so long. Now a wave of immense relief washed over her soul, replacing her great burden with an indescribable peace.

Big Lake Resort sat nestled in Williamsville, Georgia, population 4,600. Overlooking the eight square mile Lake William, the five-star attraction featured the Appalachian Mountains as backdrop while offering Golf and Spa amenities. With great conference facilities, the resort was a perfect mountain getaway for private party and corporate events.

Pulling up into the big circle drive lined with hedges, cars were routed to the right of the hotel to the banquet halls. The limos dropped off the kids at the entrance of the giant ballroom where a royal welcome awaited them. Parents, friends and volunteers lined the entrance behind brass stanchions, cheering loudly for each kid as they walked down the red carpet. Camera bulbs flashed and the smiles were non-stop while the kids stopped along the walkway to sign autographs and take pictures with their adoring fans, most of whom happened to be classmates or relatives.

Adjacent to the main ballroom was an indoor theatre that hosted concert events, but tonight was set up so parents could watch the dance on a live feed via three big screens and be close enough for any medical emergencies. The live DJ cranked the speakers loud enough that you could hear the music every time a Ballroom door opened, but the volume in the theatre was turned down so the parents could talk among themselves.

Inside the theatre, Maria became animated, pointing at the middle screen. "Look, there's our Suzy. She looks so beautiful."

Smiling once he spotted his daughter, Brian prayed out loud, "Thank you God, that Suzy's feet are feeling good and she can attend this amazing event."

"Amen. Thank you, Lord." Maria added, squeezing her husband's hand.

On the ballroom dance floor, Suzy congregated with her other classmates and their escorts. Not surprising to her parents, she soon challenged Tim to a dance off.

"Tim, I bet I can dance better than you," she bragged, yelling over the music.

"Those are mighty bold words, Suzy. Let's see what you got," Tim said, holding his chin in judgment.

"Do you know the typewriter?" Suzy asked and started pretending like she was sitting in front of a typewriter and moving her fingers to an invisible keyboard.

"Hope you got something a little more exciting," Tim shouted back, then pretended to type with one hand while covering a fake yawn with his other hand.

"Oh yeah? What about the Sprinkler?" Suzy asked, extending her arm outward, waving it side to side, and imitating a lawn water sprinkler.

Staring up at the screen inside the theatre, Brian and Maria looked at each other and started laughing out loud. "Uh oh, here we go. Poor Tim has no idea what he's about to get into," Brian said, grinning.

Tim acted like he was brushing dust off his shoulder. "Pffttttt...I practically invented the Sprinkler, girl. This is how you do it." Tim cocked one hand behind his head with the elbow perpendicular to his shoulders and the other arm extended straight out, waving it horizontally and acting as if he sprayed all the kids.

Suzy laughed. "That's good, Tim. What about the lawn mower?" Suzy began pretending to yank on a push lawnmower cord to start it before pushing the mower across the floor while wiggling her hips.

"One of my all-time favs! But back up, because this is how it's done." Tim mimicked Suzy's same exact moves except he got even more exaggerated with the hips as he strutted in front of them. Once he came to a stop in front of Suzy, he slanted his head to the side cockily, gesturing that he knew his last move had left his date impressed.

"Well, now you back up cause you gonna see the Electric Lobster!" Suzy took three quick steps and launched herself into a Pete Rose slide across the wooden floor. Coming to a stop, she started writhing on the floor in random spasmodic moves before popping back onto her feet. Her face was now covered in sweat and Tim stared at her in disbelief.

"I, uh, cannot say I know that one," Tim laughed, not wanting to duplicate the move.

"Can you break dance?" Suzy asked and before he could answer, Suzy was on the floor, attempting to balance herself on one arm while she pivoted around in several quick circles before finishing with a three hundred and sixty degree spin on her back.

Tim started clapping and then reached down to help her off the floor. "We have our winner!" he exclaimed, which caused the rest of her classmates to start jumping up and down and high fiving one another. The dance-off helped break the ice and now the other kids started boogying themselves.

Those inside the theatre who were tuned into the middle screen and witnessed the dance off were laughing hysterically and Brian hoped he could get a video copy of the event.

At the end of the dance, Tim walked Suzy out to meet her parents in the courtyard beside the Ballroom.

"Well, hats off to Suzy for taking me down in a dance contest," Tim said, wiping some sweat off his forehead.

"We saw it on the big screen, Tim. She actually took it easy on you, but we knew you didn't stand a chance," Brian said, laughing.

"I had a blast, Suzy. Thank you so much for making me smile all night," Tim said, reaching over and hugging her.

"We appreciate you so much, Tim. I almost hated to beat you at the golf event. Almost," Brian quipped.

"Geez…. you beat me at golf. Your daughter beat me at dancing. This family is seriously dangerous." Tim laughed.

"Let the man go get some rest," Maria interrupted, reaching over to hug Tim. "Thank you for making this night so awesome for all these kids. You are a huge blessing to all of us."

"Glad y'all made it out because I'm the one who gets blessed. Unfortunately, I need to hurry to get back to Atlanta tonight for a flight to New York. Let me get another hug from Suzy before I leave."

As Tim walked away toward the waiting Limo, Suzy yelled out, "Tim, you can come to my Birthday party."

Turning around and walking backward, Tim yelled, "That sounds awesome, Suzy. Send me an invite."

"Ok. I will!" Suzy exclaimed, and released the final high kick of the night.

Desperately wanting to see and talk to her husband about everything that just transpired, Sherry decided to forsake the game and drive back home. This conversation could not wait till tomorrow.

Sherry texted her Assistant Cheer Coach, Melissa, informing her that something personal came up and she would not be coming to Colbert County.

When she arrived at home, Sherry found Dave on the couch watching a basketball game replay, as usual. Hearing her open the door, he looked back over his shoulder, surprised, saying, "Why aren't you at the football game?"

Sherry let out a big breath. "Babe, I need to talk. I didn't want to wait another minute."

The seriousness of her tone caused him to turn the television off and slide over on the couch to make more room for her. "What's going on?"

"Oh my. So much has happened in the last few hours that my head is spinning. But first I need to tell you that I have been hiding something from you and I feel awful about that." Sherry's eyes dropped.

Dave ran his hand through his hair, bracing himself for the news.

Realizing her husband's mind must be all over the place with how she just phrased that, Sherry wanted to quickly clarify and help put him more at ease. "I've been worried and confused the last two weeks because I've been waiting for some test results on the baby. I didn't tell you because I didn't want you to worry and honestly, I wasn't sure what to think about what the Doctor was saying." Sherry paused, trying to gather strength to tell him. Her eyes watered and her voice became scratchy as she tried to force the words out. "But I got the tests…." Sherry's emotions got the best of her and now her throat became too constricted to keep talking.

He reached over to hold his wife's hand. "Just relax, honey." Dying to know the results, Dave also felt compelled to share what was on his own heart.

"I need to confess something to you," he said, looking her in the eyes.

His statement caught her off guard, changing the direction of the conversation.

"I haven't been up front about my own recent confusion and doubts. I've been praying like crazy lately, day and night for you and the baby. But I had two dreams that just totally rocked me. I didn't know what to make of them and well, last night I had a third dream that I feel confirmed the other two. I know this might scare you, but I have to tell you."

Sherry's eyes were wide, wondering where all this mysticism was coming from and where it was possibly headed.

Tears also formed in Dave's eyes and he took a deep breath before speaking. "Sherry, I think our child is gonna have Down Syndrome."

Sherry nodded, tears now flowing down her face, but not out of pain.

"Babe, that's what I came home to tell you. I got the test results today. Your dream is from God. Our baby is gonna have Downs."

Dave put his arms around his wife and pulled her close to him as they wept.

While before the fear of even having this discussion had overwhelmed both of them, their conversation turned liberating as it reminded them that God was indeed in control.

After wiping her face, Sherry told him about her stop at the boat launch. "I prayed sincerely for the first time in six months. It's like I have been in this heavy fog bank for so long and the sunlight came bursting forth. On the way home, I found a Christian music station and just worshipped my heart out. I can't even explain how good it felt to reconnect with God."

"That's what I've been praying for mostly, Sherry. I knew you needed to be restored. And I know our baby is going to be a huge gift. I'm already in love with this child," Dave said, resting his hand on her belly.

"I've been agonizing for two weeks about this day and now it honestly feels like the best day ever. I still can't believe it, but I am at total peace with how the pregnancy will turn out," Sherry said while sniffing, but let out a soft laugh. "And it just hit me how incredibly hungry I am right now."

Dave stood up, pulling Sherry along with him and said, "Let's go down to Rosco's for some Barbeque. I'll even buy."

"Ha! And I will tell you about how I hung out with Tim Tebow at school today while you got your oil changed."

Dave purposefully exaggerated the shock by dropping his jaw as far as his mouth could open before asking slowly, "What in tarnation are you even talking about?"

"Dave, it's been a long, interesting day. I'm starving so let's go and I will tell you all about it on the drive over there."

Chapter 8

For some reason, almost every Sunday morning seemed like a struggle for the Beckham's household to get out the door on time for church. Suzy didn't make things easy and usually changed clothes at least twice, sometimes by choice, sometimes by pouring too much ketchup on her eggs, such as she did this morning.

Only Daniel never appeared hurried, sitting on the couch watching ESPN and waiting for his parents to head toward the car.

Fortunately, there was a second service at 10:30 am at Gilmerton First Baptist or the Beckhams may never have attended church. Somehow arriving ten minutes early made this day feel like a miracle as they walked into church, greeting friends and some ushers before worship started.

One of the original buildings in Gilmerton, the rectangular white brick chapel featured the traditional steeple in the front of the building. Tall, stained-glass windows engraved with Biblical themed stories lined the side walls of the church, providing natural light and spiritual reminders.

The Beckhams liked that the Southern tradition of dressing up was not strictly followed at their home church. While several of the elders still wore their Sunday best, and Pastor Gil always wore a tie, there wasn't a sense that people were dressing to impress here.

Entering the sanctuary, the Beckhams noticed most of the pews were already filled with people. The church could hold approximately three hundred people sitting side by side, but people usually left a gap between family members. As they walked down the center aisle, halfway down they found an empty pew. With Suzy leading the way, the family started filing in down the row, only to notice at the other end sat a lone woman with her Labrador. While the dog looked relaxed and lay at her feet, the woman sat rigidly, chewing on her nails, looking uneasy and out of place.

Suzy became extremely excited, turning back to Maria and saying, "Look Mama, there's Lucy and Alice," before rushing down the aisle to pet the dog.

Alice smiled at Suzy's familiar and friendly face, acknowledging her parents and sibling with a nod.

Walking down the outside aisle in front of the stained-glass windows was the new usher, Ted, who recently moved to Gilmerton a few months ago. After spotting the dog, he leaned down and begin whispering to Alice. When she would not comply, he said out loud, "Ma'am, you can't have your dog in here."

With many eyes in the congregation now staring at her, Alice's face turned beet red and Maria could not tell if she was simply embarrassed or angry or both.

As she petted Lucy, Suzy looked up at the usher and asked "Why not? I like this doggy."

"Ma'am, I'm sorry, but this is brand new carpet in here. We simply can't have a dog messing it up," Ted insisted, just as Pastor Gil came walking hurriedly up behind him.

Gil gently grabbed Ted by the arm and whispered to his usher that it was ok and to let the dog stay.

Ted shrugged his shoulders and walked toward the back while Gil looked down, smiling at his two new guests.

Sensing the Pastor was standing next to her, she reluctantly turned her head toward Gil and when she caught his eyes, he stood at attention, placing his right hand over his eyebrow and saluted her.

"Captain Alice Murray, it is indeed an honor to have you in our presence. Please let us know if we can be of service to you or your beautiful dog. And may God shine His face upon you this morning!"

Alice nodded back in silence, looking uncomfortable that Pastor Gil had broadcast her military rank.

After Brian heard his Pastor say her full name out loud, he remembered the story about Captain Alice Brown, surprised to learn it was the same homeless lady he always saw around town.

A decorated Iraq war hero, Captain Brown's helicopter had been shot down, killing everyone else aboard while seriously injuring her back. Struggling on and off with pain medicine addiction for years, Alice could never get past the pain of being the lone survivor of the crash.

As Brian contemplated her story as a wounded vet, a rush of compassion swept over him; he started praying that God would heal her heart. While Brian prayed silently for Alice during the announcements, Maria's eyes darted around to the pews in front of her, looking for any of her friends from her Bible study group.

During worship, everyone remained seated and somewhat subdued. All but one. Buster was feeling it this morning, swaying back and forth during the entire worship service. He never stopped waving his hands toward Heaven and just as Brian had said, sang louder than the choir. Suzy chuckled watching her friend basically take over the front of the church.

Pastor Gil came to the altar and delivered a heartfelt message about the Good Samaritan and how we need to have a servant's heart to all those we encounter. Probably wondering what some of his board members and elders thought about allowing the dog to stay on their new carpet, Gil decided at the end to add a story to his planned sermon.

"In conclusion, I want to tell you an amazing story about a famous Pastor on the West Coast. Now even though he wasn't Baptist, he was still a top-notch preacher." Gil's joke elicited a laugh from his congregation.

"But this pastor was preaching during this wild revival period in the 70s out in California when all these hippies were coming in droves to Jesus. And these free-spirited hippies were coming in as they were: long-haired and barefoot. And this alarmed many of the regular church goers. They got very concerned and told the Pastor, 'Hey, all these new guys comin' in here with their dirty feet are gonna destroy our carpet.'

"And the Pastor agreed with his congregation and said, 'You are right, this carpet is gonna get ruined'."

"And the ushers said, 'Ok then, we will tell these hippies not to come in unless they got shoes on'."

"But the Pastor shook his head and said, 'Oh no. I meant we better get rid of this carpet. Don't be keeping out the people God invited in here.'"

Ted the Usher stood along the back wall and upon hearing the story, he smiled and nodded in approval at his Pastor.

"You guys have a blessed day in The Lord, and we will see you next Sunday." Pastor Gil finished.

Brian glanced over to see if the sermon had changed Alice's demeanor, but she seemed to still be on guard.

Maria stood up, saying to her kids, "You guys wanna go out for some lunch?"

Suzy started petting the dog again and shouted at her parents, "Hey, can Lucy and Alice come to lunch with us?"

Brian smiled at Suzy and said, "Yes, Alice you are welcome to join us for lunch at Jack's Fish Camp if you would like."

Alice nodded no and said, "Thank you, but I have to go."

"Awww. Next week?" Suzy asked, looking up at her.

"Maybe. Maybe next time," she said, smiling at Suzy.

"Yes, we hope to see you next week then Alice." Brian added

"Make sure you bring Lucy, ok?" Suzy said.

"I will. I might come back just to see you," Alice added.

Now standing behind her, Pastor Gil held a yellow envelope in one hand. "Hi Alice, can I have a few minutes to talk with you before you leave?"

Alice turned around and nodded, "Sure, Gil. I can talk."

Wanting to give his Pastor and Alice some privacy, Brian waved his family to follow him down the pew to the center aisle. Grateful that Gil was going to offer her some assistance on the church's behalf, Brian walked out of the chapel content, believing Alice would have a chance at getting some help she needed.

Besides the temperate climate, the other reason North Georgia remains so lush is the large amount of rain the area receives. But what makes for beautiful forests can also make it maddening for those who enjoy the outdoors. Like the past week when torrential downpour kept everybody in Gilmerton stuck indoors, causing many to go stir crazy.

The weather forecast continued to look bleak through the next weekend and unfortunately threatened to cancel the last football game of the season and Suzy's chance to finally cheer.

Despite the foul weather, several Cheerleaders looked for Suzy during lunch on Thursday to present her with a gift. Approaching her group table, they witnessed her pour copious amounts of Ketchup on a corndog. Amanda led the way, holding a bag behind her back while Suzy remained so focused on her food that she didn't notice any of them until the squad surrounded her.

"Hey Suz, we got something for you," Amanda said.

"I'm eating a corndog," Suzy said, holding the evidence up for all to see.

Amanda laughed and said, "We can see that. Do you want a present?"

"Ok. But my birthday is in July," Suzy said.

The squad was confident Suzy's lackadaisical attitude was about to change.

Hearing from their coach about the girls' plan, Billy had kept the secret and now sat at the end of the lunch table, eager to see Suzy's reaction.

"Well, we wanted you to have this. You earned it," Amanda said, pulling the surprise from behind her and presenting Suzy with an official West End Cheerleader uniform.

Suzy's mouth went wide in shock and she was unable to speak for a few seconds. She soon recovered and went into full spaz mode, thrusting herself out of the chair. Suzy hopped up and down, screaming, and caused the entire lunchroom to look over at her table. Laughing at Suzy's reaction, Amanda handed the uniform to her, watching Suzy hold it in her arms like a newborn baby.

"Look, Mister Billy. Ima cheerleader!" Suzy yelled to her teacher, showing him the treasured gift.

"That you are Miss Suzy. It is official now. What do you say to the team?" Billy pointed to the girls around her.

"Thank you, guys," Suzy said, making it to each cheerleader and giving all of them hugs.

"Hopefully, it won't rain tomorrow night so we can cheer together. But wear it to school tomorrow anyway, ok Suzy? Amanda instructed.

Friday afternoon came and the rain continued throughout the day as predicted. Suzy happily wore the new cheer uniform to school, showing it off to all her classmates, but after returning home her demeanor changed, and the usually bubbly attitude now mirrored the gray skies.

Hearing her dad on the phone, she was saddened to learn that her grandparents in Tennessee would not be making the drive down to see the game due to the nasty weather. Worry took over and she constantly peered outside the living room window, hoping to see the rain cease.

An hour and half later, a short break in the downpour caused Suzy to get excited and she yelled to her Dad in his office that the rain had stopped. He didn't want Suzy to get her hopes up, but the radar forecast on his cell phone said there might be a clearing of rain clouds after all.

Finally, at 6:30 PM the family gathered to leave for the game; it had not rained for the past hour.

The entire town of Gilmerton was excited to see the 25th year rival game between West End and Independent High. A win would not only give West End the edge in the series, but leave them with a winning season.

As the Beckhams piled out thru the front door of the house with their rain gear, Suzy stopped, her face grimacing and said, "My feet are hurting. Can't go."

Brian and Maria looked at each other with wide eyes, distressed to hear the foot problem had returned.

"Just kidding!" Suzy laughed. "Let's go."

"Suzy! Don't mess with us like that, girl!" Maria said, shaking her head.

"I thought it was funny, Suzy," Brian chimed in. "What about you, Daniel?"

"It was semi-funny. But the look on y'all's faces was definitely funny," Daniel added.

"Well, let's hurry and get over to the stadium," Brian said.

The wind grew calm and while the temperature was still brisk at fifty-three degrees, the low cloud cover kept the night air warmer than usual for November.

As planned, Suzy and her mom met Coach Sherry at the gate inside the stadium near the end zone to let her onto the field. Once Suzy greeted her coach, she bolted down the track to join the rest of the squad, causing Maria and Sherry to chuckle.

"Wow, I guess someone is a little excited," Sherry said.

"Coach, we wanted to thank y'all for getting her the uniform. She actually did sleep in it last night and I will be shocked if she takes it off for a week."

"That's, too, cute. The girls really wanted her to have it."

Maria reached over and touched the coach's elbow. "Hey, I also wanted to share something really quick with you. I can't really explain this, but as I prayed the other day, I mean, first of all I've never had this kind of experience, but I feel God is leading me to tell you that whatever you are going through right now, it's all gonna work out."

Sherry's eyes blurred with tears and she patted her hand on her heart. "Oh my goodness. How I need to talk to you. I'm the one. I'm the friend I was trying to tell you about at the Bagel shop. I'm the one who is pregnant with a Down's baby."

Sherry's emotion proved contagious and Maria's throat tightened, fighting back her own tears. She leaned forward and hugged Sherry. "Oh amiga, you are about to be blessed beyond your imagination." Maria pulled back and looked at her in the eyes. "My family is gonna be here for you on this journey."

Grateful for the new friend she had in Maria, she said, "Thank you so much for telling me that. I need that positive affirmation and I now know you were put in my path for a reason."

"Look, I want you and your husband to come over for dinner tomorrow night. Can you make it?" Maria asked.

"We can. I look forward to it," Sherry said, smiling.

"Great. I'll let you get over to your team. We can talk more later," Maria said, starting to walk over to the stadium.

Along the railing in front of stadium seats stood six of the Magnificent Seven, eagerly waiting to see their friend's dream come true. In fact, many of the student body were in the stands also looking forward to their classmate's Cheerleading debut. But the game had just started, and Suzy was nowhere to be found.

Sitting on the second row with Daniel, Maria and Brian looked at each other, wondering where their daughter could be.

A mysterious refrigerator sized box sat next to the stands, draped in gift wrap with a giant bow on top. At the five-minute mark of the first quarter, the entire cheerleading squad of twenty girls ran over to the box, appearing to lift and shuffle it back over to the sidelines. This pre-planned move cued the PA announcer to come over the intercom and say, "Can I have your attention. Will West End High School please give a warm welcome to our newest Cheerleader, Suzy Beckham!"

The Cheerleading squad ripped the sides of the box open, revealing their newest member. Suzy stepped forward, waving at everyone with her black and blue pom poms, and the crowd erupted in applause.

Just as Sherry's husband Dave suggested, the girls designed special cheer formations for Suzy. One of them, called 'The Tunnel', had the girls line up opposite each other, extending their arms and pompoms toward the other cheerleader and forming the roof of a makeshift tunnel. Obscured from view, Suzy ran down through the tunnel and exploded out to face the crowd, finishing with her trademark high kick.

Exciting the entire Magnificent Seven crew, Buster got her classmates chanting 'Suzy, Suzy, Suzy'. Within a minute, the chant was being repeated in the stands and the town of Gilmerton now rooted loudly for the local favorite. Brian put his arm around his wife, touched by the outpouring of love and affection for their daughter.

Coach Sherry walked out to meet her newest team member and presented a giant megaphone with Suzy's name painted on the side in school colors. No one could predict the entertaining comedy and antics the bullhorn would soon provide, save her closest family members who knew Suzy could improvise like nobody's business.

After sticking to the script of having Suzy lead the Victory chant where the crowd repeated each letter of the word, Suzy began creating her own cheers on the fly.

Right before half time, Suzy walked closer to stands and began barking a cheer into her bullhorn:

"Hey Mom   Hey Dad

Get off   Your Seat

Go get   Some Food

I want   To Eat"

The crowd erupted in laughter while her parents sat chuckling and shaking their heads.

This solo cheer got the entire student section repeating it, even chanting it later in the parking lot.

Thinking their daughter was joking, her parents continued sitting there until Suzy walked closer, yelling into the bullhorn as if she was on her own private communication device, "Mama, serious. I'm hungry. Can you get me a hamburger?"

Maria blushed, but nodded yes to let Suzy know she would indeed get her some food.

Just above Suzy in the bleachers stood Olivia Taylor along with her soccer teammates. One of Suzy's math tutors, Olivia had come to see Suzy's debut and yelled below now that she was within ear shot. "Hey, Suzy, you are doing great. I love you!"

"Thanks, Hotdog," Suzy shouted back her nickname for Olivia thru the bullhorn. "I love you, too. But right now, I gotta go cheer for my boys." She turned and scampered back over to the sidelines.

Hearing the strange nickname, Olivia's friends exploded in laughter.

West End High School was on the fortunate end of a wet field, taking advantage of five fumbles by Independent High and went into the fourth quarter with a three-touchdown lead. Comfortable with the score, the Wildcats coach inserted mostly second-string players into the game which kept the hometown crowd relaxed and able to just enjoy the Suzy Show.

While her squad still displayed some of their high-performance cheers that would give them a chance to compete at Nationals, Sherry allowed Suzy to freelance up and down the sidelines, knowing it created a more fun atmosphere. Coach was proud of her team for embracing Suzy and not being concerned that she had created her own stage. Which was good, because somebody was just getting warmed up.

The longer the game went on, the less Suzy's cheers had to do with the team or football. She even borrowed lyrics from pop and rap songs she knew, and despite their irrelevance to the game, the crowd didn't care and ate up all the spontaneous cheers Suzy created.

Marching in front of the stands, Suzy blasted thru the megaphone toward the opposing team: "Comb your hair, brush your teeth, wash your feet, they really stink!"

The last crowd pleaser caused Daniel to laugh and turn to his parents, saying "Uh, oh. Suzy's gone full on rogue now." And he wasn't wrong.

Lifting the personal Bullhorn to her lips, Suzy incited the crowd to follow along and they repeated after her:

"Give me a K, give me a E, give me a T, give me a C, give me a H, give me a U, give me a P. What's that spell?" Suzy shouted.

The whole crowd screamed back, "Ketchup"!"

After the game, Coach Sherry held her arm around Suzy's shoulder, escorting her over to her parents who waited at the gate by the end zone.

Knowing she had gotten into her own little world on the sidelines, Daniel decided to tease his sister, asking her "Who won the game, Suzy?"

"I don't know. I cheer. I don't play football." She shook her head, not believing she had to explain it to her brother.

"Fair enough," Daniel replied.

Maria said to Sherry, "Coach, sorry about Suzy going off script there. We had a feeling she might get a little carried away."

"Don't worry about it. This game was perfect for it. In fact, as I watched her, I thought about how uniform and rigid I can be. How I want everything to go as I planned. It reminded me I need to go with the flow more and just be ready for the curveballs life throws at us."

Maria nodded in agreement, having the insight of what Sherry was experiencing after their pregame talk.

Brian noticed Suzy's face had turned downcast, so he leaned down and asked her, "What's wrong, Snuzer?"

Shaking her head in disappointment and letting out a big breath, Suzy said, "No more cheering. Last game."

Sherry reached down and gave Suzy a hug. "What are you talking about? We still have Basketball season coming up?"

"Yes!" Suzy pumped her fist in the air as her face now beamed with joy. "Mama, Ima still a cheerleader!"

"Yes, hija, I told you. You will always be a cheerleader." Maria said.

A humid summer heat wave welcomed the first week of June and Billy was grateful for his air- conditioned classroom. The last day of school was bittersweet as he hated knowing he would no longer see his senior students, but at the same time he was excited for them as they began the next chapter of their life.

"Good morning, Magnificent Seven! This has been an amazing year! And I have some amazing news before we even start the class. I just got word that earlier this morning Coach Sherry gave birth to a seven-pound baby boy named Isaac."

Suzy screamed, bounding out of her seat and kicked for the heavens. "Yes. I love babies!"

Billy chuckled as Suzy sat back down. "Yes. Who doesn't love babies? Ok, I look forward to our last day together and I want to thank you guys for making these past fours so awesome for me. I hope all of you will stay in touch and let me know how y'all are doing. I decided that today we will finish this year the way we started. I know some of you guys have new dreams now and I want to go around the room and hear what some of your hopes and dreams are. Let's start with my main man, Justin."

Today was one of the few times over the past year Justin did not have a clothing item related to Star Wars. Instead he donned a red NASA t-shirt and Georgia Tech baseball cap. Rocking back and forth slowly in his wheelchair, Justin said, "Mr. Billy, I am going to be an astrophysicist and build a spaceship for my wheelchair so I can be an astronaut."

Billy raised his hands up in the air. "That's what I'm talking about, Justin. We cannot wait to see you launch off to space one day. Class, you may not know, but Justin received a scholarship to study astrophysics at Georgia Tech. So let's give him a round of applause as he gets ready to fly."

Justin smiled proudly and the kids followed Billy's lead of clapping to congratulate him.

"Now, let's hear from Mister Earl Smith himself. Are you still going to be cutting the rug with those amazing dance skills?"

Earl had not stopped clapping for Justin and became excited to share his own dream.

"My mom told me Dan Aykroyd from Ghost Busters also had Asperger's so I want to be an actor now, too," he said.

"Well, I look forward to seeing you not only on the big stage with those fancy dance moves but on the big screen with those acting skills one day, Earl."

Sliding over to the red hair and freckled student, Billy noticed the one word printed across his t-shirt read 'Joy'. "Now, Mister Buster, that shirt is beyond appropriate because you have been nothing but a joy to have in my class. Do I have to even ask or is it still your dream to be a Preacher?"

"Yes. My dad said I can help. With kindergarten class. At church." Stuttering slightly, he finished, "I, I, I can't wait."

"I love it. You are going to do awesome things, Buster. Keep the faith, my man," Billy said, before walking over and standing between the desks of Katie and Josh.

"Okay, cutie Katie. Besides helping your mom run the salon, what are your other dreams?"

"I'm learn make dresses with my grandma," she replied.

"That's great, Katie. What about you Josh? Wait, is your hair painted like a watermelon?

Only seeing Josh's hair before from a distance, Billy thought Josh just had a random combo of green on top and pink on the sides until he noticed the black spots representing seeds.

"Yes, Katie's mom helped color it yesterday at her shop. Do you like it?"

"Like it? I love it. Watermelon is my favorite. Please, for all things sacred, let me take a picture of it after class," Billy said chuckling. "Now what are some of your dreams for the future?"

"I wanna learn to play piano," Josh said, pretending to push piano keys on his desk.

"Wow, you are really expanding your musical tastes. That is great!"

"And I wanna marry Katie," Josh said, causing his teacher's eyes to bug out. He then turned in his chair to face Katie. "You marry me?"

Turning to Josh, she replied, "Okay."

"Whoa guys," was all Billy could say, as Josh rejoiced by pumping his fist in the air while the other students became enthusiastic at the news.

Buster blurted out, "I can marry you" while Suzy shouted out, "I wanna come to the wedding!"

Taken aback, but wanting to regain control of his class, Billy said, "Ok, ok, guys, let's settle down. Remember, we can't get too loud and only one person can talk at time, even if it is the last day."

Katie raised her hand as she spoke. "Mister Billy, I forgot to say. My other dream is marry Josh. And paint his hair," she said, giggling. "But I need ask my mom."

"Yes. That's right. You guys both need talk to your parents. Ok. Whew... .y'all just blew my mind. I did not see that coming," Billy answered, shaking his head as he moved over in front of Suzy and tried to recover from hearing the impromptu marriage proposal in his class.

"So Miss Beckham, what are your dreams, hopes and aspirations? Are you still going to be a cheerleader?"

"No, I did that. Remember?" Suzy held out her palms

Smiling back at her and holding his chin, Billy replied, "Yes, I seem to remember now."

"I wanna have a house. I wanna be a babysitter for Coach Sherry. I wanna get married. And I wanna adopt a baby!" Suzy said with a big smile.

She paused so Billy replied, "Well, that's quite a list...." before Suzy cut him off by yelling out,

"And I wanna be a teacher!" She threw her hands up in the air to celebrate.

Billy reached over and gave her a high five. "My Miss Suzy, you already are. You have been teaching me since day one."

About the Author

William (Billy). Barnard has authored A Walk by The Water and fiction work The Ancestors before writing The Legend of Suzy High Kick. His work strives to not only entertain, but be thought provoking and enrich the lives of the readers.

He currently resides in San Diego, CA with his family and daughter Suzy who inspired the book.

Printed in the United States
By Bookmasters